Never Ending Circles

Reformed offender turned criminologist and writer, David Honeywell, shares his life story

David Honeywell

Published by Nocton Publishing,
25 Fawcus Court, Redcar,
Cleveland, TS10 5QX, England

http://nocton-publishing.com

ISBN 978-0-9572599-0-4

British Library Cataloguing in Publication Data.
A catalogue record for this book is available from the British
Library

Printed and bound by CPI Group (UK) Ltd, Croydon, CR0 4YY

Cover design by Stephen G. Nicholls
www.coastalviewandmoornews.co.uk

Cover photograph by Discovery Photography
www.discoveryphotography.co.uk

CONTENTS

To My Friend
e Matial arts Colleague

David Marequell

17/4/2012

ACKNOWLEDGMENTS

To my friends and family who have supported me throughout my troubled life and my decision to share my story. A big thank you to my mother who is my best friend and has never stopped supporting me throughout everything. And also to my sister Carol who has always been there for me from when we were growing up together to this very day.

Always close to my heart is my late Uncle Donald who encouraged me to study and use the pen rather than the sword. Had it not been for his influence, I doubt I would have ever entered university.

Finally, I would like to thanks all those who have knowingly and unknowingly helped me turn my life around.

David Honeywell

March 2012

PUBLISHER'S NOTE

The author has changed the names of various people in the story that follows and it is not intended that any such individuals should be recognised, criticised or otherwise referred to in a personal or real life capacity. *Never Ending Circles* contains a number of words that can best be described as prison slang. The prison glossary at the back of the book may assist any reader who is perplexed.

It aims to offer encouragement to others who have had similar experiences and now wish to turn their lives around. And that David's story of crime, carrying knives and alcohol abuse, will help deter some young people from falling into the same life of self- destruction as he did, which ruins so many lives, he says.

It has three main objectives in mind. Firstly, because ordinary people can relate to ordinary people's lives, David hopes it will go some way towards helping others who may also suffer from mental health issues as he did.

Secondly, it can show young people how much crime can ruin their lives, by showing them the lifetime of struggles and torment he has had to endure as a result of his thoughtless actions which started as a youth. Thirdly, it is aimed at students and practitioners of criminology and other disciplines to use as a textbook to further their understanding of a person's criminal and anti-social behaviour.

Note:
If you would like to contact the author directly, please email: **david.honeywell@yahoo.co.uk**

INTRODUCTION

My life hasn't been an easy one, but most of my problems have been of my own making. The title of my book refers to a life of never ending circles which describes a continual cycle of crime, prison, admissions into psychiatric institutions, alcohol abuse, self-harm, and just living within a vicious circle of repeat offending and self destruction.

But also how so many things have come full circle such as when I would one day be sat reporting for the local newspaper in the courts I was once a defendant. And how I would one day give a lecture to criminology students where I was once a student, and when the City of York where I was first arrested in 1983 would one day honour me by making me a freeman of the City. There are so many instances like this where I have come back to a place I had been before but under very different circumstances.

I talk frankly and openly about my life journey, of my time in and out of institutions, why I was incapable of holding down employment for many years, forming lasting relationships, and how I developed an alcohol addiction. I recount the many years I suffered with depression which plagued me from the tender age of fifteen. My story paints a powerful picture about a life of incarceration.

And although prison was something that actually happened to me - in the broader sense - the whole story is like a prison. It's a story of paranoia and persecution, walls closing in, the nature of oppression of the social hierarchy - about being imprisoned in oneself -

1

how I experienced all of these things and how I dealt with them.

I was inspired to write this after the riots broke out across Britain in August 2011. In the wake of this devastation, many heated debates arose and questions were raised about disaffected youth, the lack of parental control in today's society, dysfunctional families, a breakdown in penal reform, zero crime deterrents, gang culture, and a need for strong role models within communities.

All of these things rang alarm bells with me so I decided to pen my own experiences in a bid to help others and put to rest many of my own demons. It's been a humbling experience writing my story, some of it daunting, some of it poignant and some of it funny.

It has brought back many forgotten memories, both good and bad. It has also been a personal learning experience in itself. I have been pleasantly surprised at the general response from the public which has been nothing but positive. I have learned a lot more about myself and it's even reunited me with many of those from my past I had lost contact with over the years.

If I could turn the clock back, I most definitely would. But as I can't, I can at least try to help others. I was aged twenty before I got my first criminal convictions for two attempted robberies resulting in a thirty month youth custody sentence. I then spent the rest of my early adult years drifting through different towns and cities and too many jobs to remember. I also committed relatively petty, mostly impulsive, but occasionally violent crimes such as criminal damage and common assault. My directionless way of life also included several periods in psychiatric hospitals for clinical depression. Then in July 1995, I was given a five year prison sentence for 'wounding with intent to cause grievous bodily harm.' I went to prison an un-educated individual with massive failings to overcome, but with a new determination to turn things around. Seven years after leaving prison, I graduated with a bachelor's degree in criminology, followed two years later with a master's degree in social research methods.

After my master's degree in 2003, I continued shaping my journalism skills writing for the university's student newspaper. Then in 2005, my first article for a regional newspaper appeared in the *York Press* (the Press) and my journalism career had begun. Since then I've been regularly writing and contributing to the *Evening Gazette, Northern Echo, the Press, Sunday Sun* and various magazines.

In 2007, my article, Our Heroes about my grandfather's heroics on the Somme, appeared in a book, *Times Past: The Story of York*, written by York Press Deputy Editor, Bill Hearld. Then in 2008, I was commissioned by Redcar and Cleveland council's 'Business Enterprise Team' to write press releases about local fledgling businesses they had funded and coached.

In 2009, I launched my own newspaper, Coastal View to give local businesses their own medium. And most recently, I have written for the Prisoner's Education Trust, UNLOCK, The National Organisation of Reformed Offenders, and the Open University as well as touring the UK university circuit giving talks about 'the prison experience' to students.

CHAPTER ONE

WHERE IT ALL BEGAN

I was born on 1 August 1963 on a Royal Air Force base called *Nocton Hall* in Lincolnshire, to Eric and Nancy Honeywell. I also have one sister, called Carol, who is five years older than me. My father was originally from Eston near Middlesbrough and my mother was from Fulford in York. Because my father was serving in the Royal Air Force, we moved around a lot from one camp to another every two or three years.

As a result of this, our schooling became quite disrupted and our lives became quite unsettled, because as soon as we'd made friends, we were off again.

Every school had a different system - teaching methods, curriculums and routines. And I seem to recall that some teachers had the attitude that because we wouldn't be there for long anyway, there wasn't a lot of point investing too much time in us.

There was also a very different attitude from certain teachers towards the kids from camp compared to the local kids who the teachers had seen through infants and primary and whose parents they had forged friendships with over the years.

I can remember these very early feelings of isolation and prejudice. We were outcasts wherever we went, but there were lots of other RAF children in our position.

Some of them had been living on camps abroad for several years and then had to suddenly readjust to life in Britain. From when I was three, we lived for about five years on a middle class housing estate in Porthcawl, South

Wales called Summerfield Drive. My father was stationed at nearby RAF St Athan.

Porthcawl holds wonderful memories for me during this period of my early childhood in the 1960s - a time I often reminisce with my mother.

I can recall my mother showing me what hippies and beatniks were and I remember those flowered coloured beetle cars they used to drive around in. It was the first time I was introduced to prejudice too. There were a lot Welsh natives who didn't much like the English, but this was just the beginning towards a lifetime of bigotry for me.

The RAF used to organise massive family events such as *Battle of Britain* displays every September where all the families could go and enjoy a gala day. We would see the *Red Arrows*, the RAF gymnastics squad and dog handler displays. We also got chance to sit inside aeroplanes and get our photographs taken. Then there would be the usual stalls and games.

And at Christmas time, they used to organise magnificent parties for all the kids. We all spent the first part of the day watching cartoons at the cinema followed by a tea party in a huge hall which had a large Christmas tree and a stack of presents in one corner for all the kids.

Santa would enter the hall on a sleigh and then each child's name was individually called out for them to go and collect their presents.

Not far from us, was a local amusement park in Porthcawl, called Coney Beach with all the rides and excitement fayres can bring. From our house, you could hear the crowds and screams from people on the rollercoaster and rides. And you could see the flashing lights everywhere. In 1971, we left Wales and moved to RAF Hullavington (now Buckley Barracks), near

Chippenham, Wiltshire. Whenever you are sent anywhere in the military, it's referred to as being 'posted'. We lived in a four-bedroom house known as a married quarter. Married quarters are houses provided for military personnel and their families to live in. When we lived in these houses, there were certain archaic rules laid down by the RAF.

In those days, all the families on camp had to use their regulation furniture, and if you marked or damaged any, you would be charged for it. We couldn't have wallpaper; we had to use their regimental green or blue paint on the walls. My father was always getting on to us kids, reminding us not to mark walls or furniture. Every time we moved house, two officials from the Department of Environment (DOE) would pay us a visit to conduct an inspection.

They would run their fingers along the door frames and shelves checking for dust and inspect for marks on the walls. I can clearly see them now slowly reading down their endless check list, examining everything in sight, from cutlery and crockery, to walls, floors and even the back garden.

On one occasion, we were all sat in the car ready to set off when the inspectors made my father go back into the garden with a spade and break the soil into smaller chunks, because they felt they were too big.

My mother said that on the day of these moves while waiting for the inspectors to turn up, she was constantly on edge with two kids running around worrying in case we marked the walls or furniture. She was even too scared to cook us dinner in case she marked the cooker. Everything in the house was grey, blue or green, including the walls and carpets. We got to see a lot of aeroplanes and activity as we lived so close to the airfields and runways. This was also a great place for us to ride our bikes in the vast free empty space. But you had to always keep a look out for the red warning lights at the gates. The Parachute Regiment used to train there and you would see soldiers, large trucks and hardware descending from *Hercules* aircraft.

When the red lights were on, you stayed off the runways. If by chance you happened to get caught halfway across when they were lit-up, the 'Snowdrops' (RAF Police), would be there in minutes to escort you off in a *Land Rover*.

In 1973, we moved to RAF Leeming in North Yorkshire and it was here that my life would start to change for the worse. I was ten-years-old and although I always kept a few select friends, I spent a lot of time in my bedroom playing records on an old-fashioned record player that had seen better days.

The Bay City Rollers were all the rage then and all my friends were wearing the latest tartan clad trousers and tops with baseball boots. Whenever I asked my father if he would buy me some clothes so I could look the same as the other kids, as always, I was abruptly refused.

This was usual for him. I remember once having to beg him for a new pair of shoes because the ones I was wearing had holes in the bottoms and my socks would get soaked on a wet day.

Families who lived on RAF camps were a mixture of all different classes. I use the term 'class' because the military always made sure people knew exactly which class they belonged to.

Lower ranks and commissioned officers families were separated into different communities on the camp. There was a real snobbery in the forces which I later came across during my stint in the army too. Whenever there was a formal invitation to a dance or a ball, the notice board would display a notice which would read something along the lines of, 'Officers will bring their ladies, warrant officers and senior ranks will bring their wives, and NCOs, (non-commissioned officers), will bring their women.'

(The definition of an NCO is an enlisted member of the armed forces, such as a corporal, sergeant, or petty officer, appointed to a rank conferring leadership over other enlisted personnel.) Not only was this sheer snobbery, but totally untrue in many cases, because some of the officer's wives were anything but ladies.

My mother used to clean houses for some of them, and she would tell me that a lot of the officer's wives wore their husbands rank - thinking they were a cut above the rest. But in fact most were very ordinary people looking down their noses at everyone else. Yet the higher in rank the officers were, the more genuine and 'down-to-earth' they and their wives seemed to be. It was as always, the 'jumped-ups' that were the worst.

My grandmother who was an army wife used to tell my mother exactly the same. I saw a real class divide on these camps and it was here I learned to despise some of the upper echelons of society and see them for what they really were.

I can remember when I was in the army; one of my mates was dating a major's daughter. One sunny Saturday afternoon, she invited me and a friend along with her boyfriend, to her home.

I could see the disapproval on her mother's patronising face as she looked down her nose at us from across their very plush living room. She then asked her daughter if she could have a word in private. I knew what was coming next. I had seen it all before, and low and behold, we were then asked to leave. It seemed hypocritical that although her daughter was allowed to date an army private, his mates were unwelcome at her home. But living in the military as a child had already opened my eyes to the unbearable snobbery amongst the ranks.

The early years were by far the happiest for me as I remember and I still look back with fond memories of South Wales, RAF Hullavington and Leeming. But I was too young to see that underneath the surface, things were not so happy at home.

My mother didn't have a very happy life with my father. Apart from being generally ill-tempered, he would often lash out at her for the slightest thing. She'd get the occasional black eye or bleeding nose which she and Carol would always try to hide from me. He was also extremely greedy and tight with money.

After bed-time, me and Carol would hear them rowing downstairs and we would lie in our beds listening - scared stiff wondering what might happen next.

CHAPTER TWO

PLAYGROUND BULLIES

It was during my secondary school days in the 1970s, I first saw someone get a good kicking from a gang, which was actually on my behalf. A gang leader who liked my sister had heard that a third year had attacked me, so he got his gang of about seven to chase him into the boys changing rooms and lay into him. I was never into being part of a gang, but seeing him get his just desserts gave me a real sense of satisfaction.

My youth was plagued by bullies who destroyed any self-esteem or confidence I ever had - which wasn't much - thanks to my father. I know many people go through this during their school years, but while some seem to get over it, others are scarred for life. And of course, some kids are bullied far worse than others.

I was an easy target. I had a mop of bright ginger hair as well as being very shy and timid. I wouldn't say 'boo to a goose' and it wasn't helped by the fact I stood out like a 'sore thumb'. Not being dressed in the fashion of the day as other kids, did little for my self confidence and made it impossible to blend in. I also wore other people's cast offs and all because my father was so tight with money. My father basically set us up for a life of misery at the hands of bullies.

One of the most important lessons I learned in life about bullies though, which would hold me in good stead for the future, was how cowardly they really are and how you should always stand up to them. It was after my transition from primary to secondary school at the age of eleven, when bullies started to target me most of all. I started to attend Bedale Secondary School in North Yorkshire when we lived at RAF Leeming. Although I've endured many other hardships in my adult life, my teenage school years were some of the most traumatic of all, because I was powerless.

Most of what happened to me later in life was of my own doing. But during my childhood years, I was an innocent victim. And of course, the bullies were still around even after the school bell had gone, because they were also my neighbours.

Overnight, I changed from being a happy child into a withdrawn, depressed, nervous wreck because of it all and the school's failure to do anything about it.

One day I begged my father to let me stay off school as I couldn't take the bullying anymore. But he forced me to go and speak to the headmaster, Mr Ramsay, with him present. I was persuaded to report the culprits after which my life became hell.

I must have looked so unhappy back then because at school one day, a lady teacher passing me on the stairs suddenly stopped me. And with a concerned expression on her face, said, 'Oh cheer up, why do you look so sad?'

I really wanted to off-load everything to her, but I had already learned the consequences of speaking out. She was one of the nicer teachers, but for many years, I blamed teachers for failing to protect me and other bullied kids like me. The ringleaders were two real losers and as always with bullies, were very different on their own.

One was a large kid who thought he was a tough nut because of his large frame and fancied himself as a football hooligan too. One day when he was taunting me in the school woodwork class I just snapped and punched him making his nose bleed. My father had been showing me the night before how I should punch him next time he picked on me. This was a turning point for me, as I now realised I was capable of standing up to bullies. I felt a sort of new confidence grow inside me after that. The taunting never went away altogether, but I always knew that when push came to shove, I could hurt someone.

It also made me aware how cowardly bullies really are. Being bullied taught me to detect weakness in them and from that day on, whenever someone pushed me too far - I lashed out.

It was difficult to concentrate on studying with all this going on, but my favourite subjects were art, music and English language. I was always able to write well from a very young age. I know full well that had it not been for such a tormented school life, I would have excelled.

One of my teachers told my parents - as all my school reports stated - that I was above average intelligence, but lacked concentration. Well what did they expect?

I also hated PT (physical training) classes or games as they were called in one school, because I wasn't good at it. The bigger, tougher kids always brow beat the weaker ones. And while the confident pupils demonstrated their sporting talents, the less confident ones were humiliated.

I would purposely leave my PT kit at home, even though I knew I would get slippered for it. I was so nervous and self conscious about my lack of sporting skills. In 1976, my father had completed his twenty two years military service so we then moved to his home town of Middlesbrough.

We lived at 12 Monmouth Road, Eston. Some would say its nearer grangetown and some would say Eston, but it's always been grangetown to me. My new school was Sarah Metcalfe Secondary. Though I was bullied at Bedale School, Sarah Metcalfe was a much rougher school. The school today (now Eston Park), is anything but like its former self when I was there. It's situated on a large field and when I was there, it was close to three other schools.

There were often running battles between each school and a constant rivalry. After my second day at Sarah Metcalfe, while on my way home, I was jumped by a gang of about six pupils from one of the other schools. I was head butted and punched to the ground, then repeatedly kicked in the face. I was with someone else and all I remember was the terrified expression on his face looking back at me as he ran like hell.

A woman was hammering on her living room window as the kicks kept coming. I was a mess and lost a tooth. But most of all I was effected psychologically and emotionally. The next day, Carol who was always a rock whenever I needed her, took me to school in search of justice. We were then sent to their school to pick them out in front of the whole class.

I recognised them immediately. My father didn't react whatsoever when he saw my cuts and bruises. He had been working that day and when he came home - I was shocked by his lack of caring.

School was a soul destroying place. Sarah Metcalfe had the reputation of enlisting some of the poorest kids from the most disadvantaged pockets of society. Here I witnessed the dreaded 'class divide' all over again.

It seemed we were looked down on by the nearby former grammar and more select schools. Those that had the confidence to excel were given the utmost encouragement and praise by teachers, while the lesser achievers were practically 'written-off'.

I didn't go back to school for most of my fifth year - I gave up on education. The school had let me down, my father had let me down and I wasn't interested in any of the subjects they taught anyway.

I couldn't believe that something like religious education could be compulsory. I hated most subjects except for those I've mentioned.

However, I had to start attending school again for the latter part of my fifth year after being warned by my teachers. Then one day, only about five of us turned up for PT because most the others were away on a school trip to Hexham.

The teacher took us over to Eston recreation ground (*the Rec*) and got us to run laps around it. And for the first time ever, I excelled. I'd found a sport, I was a natural at and was even encouraged by the teacher for once, who shouted, 'Go on Honeywell, you'll be a champ one day.'

Although this was a 'tongue in cheek' remark, it was enough to change me. It boosted my self-confidence enormously and from that day onwards, I have continued to run to this very day.

I also started using weights and joining in other fitness activities at the local sports hall which until then, I had always avoided at all costs. I was also spurned on to start using weights because one day I took a severe beating from a bigger kid who was a regular gym user. He actually became my first training partner.

The academic side of things was not so good. During exam week, I walked in to the school hall one day where other pupils were taking their places at the rows of tables. But instead of joining them, I just took one look - turned around, left, and never went back. I wouldn't have passed a thing anyway because I'd been playing truant for most of that year. Unbelievably though - ever since that day when we were made to run around the recreation ground, my most feared subject which was PT - would become a way of life for me.

Two years later, when I joined the army, I was super fit and one of the most confident soldiers in the gym. I confidently climbed the ropes, was able to clear the wooden horse, climb the wall frames and stay ahead of all the others on every single platoon run.

I achieved the highest ever fitness score during basic training and years later, I fulfilled a lifelong ambition to become a qualified fitness instructor.

What a difference one teacher's remark can make to a child's self-esteem.

CHAPTER THREE

FAMILY BLUES

After we moved to Middlesbrough, tension had now started to build at home as my father struggled to adapt to civilian life. He became even more unpredictable and struggled to hold down a job. Then not long after - Carol and I were both hit with a bombshell!

My parents sat us both down and announced they were getting divorced. I remember Carol bursting into tears and I just sat there stunned. I didn't cry because I was always taught, 'boys don't cry'.

Things had been going downhill for a while since my dad left the forces as he struggled to settle, but there had been problems for many years. And the only reason my parents had stayed together for as long as they did, was because my mother didn't want us kids to suffer a family break-up. There were many occasions she should have just left my father. And had it not been for the RAF persuading her not to divorce him years earlier - this would have happened a long time sooner.

I remember as a child always being terrified of my mother leaving us. I was always begging her not to run away. I know sometimes when she had a row with my dad; she would wander off for hours just to get some space. I developed huge insecurities over this thinking she would never come back.

Although I knew my parents had their fair share of problems over the years, the break up was still a huge shock to us. The worst part for me was being made to choose which parent I wanted to stay with. Given that my mother was the good parent, my choice was obvious.

But my father wanting to see my mother out on the streets, bullied me into verbally choosing who I wanted to stay with. One day he took me to see my grandmother not far away, then on the way back, he suddenly pulled the car over to the side of the road. He looked at me and said, 'You have to choose which one of us you want to stay with now!' I felt tormented and confused.

Then one night when I was sat in my bedroom, he came in demanding I make a decision. But my mother was there this time and told him to stop pressurising me. At that point he punched her in the side of her head and she fell on to my bed. I blurted out that I was staying with my mother.

I had never seen a man hit a woman until then. I was always taught you never hit girls. It was a massive shock to me. I ran outside to get my sister but she wasn't in. Then from across the road, I saw a police officer leaving someone's house. I ran over and told him what had happened. But he just said, 'Sorry but we don't get involved in domestics'.

My father treated me like dirt after that night. One evening, we were both sat in the living room watching television. He was now giving me permanent silent treatment. I had been to the dentist that day to have some teeth extracted and was feeling unwell from the effects of the gas.

I suddenly spewed up all over the living room floor. He just sat there without saying a single word and watched me scrub my vomit up. When my father was in a bad mood, he used to always take it out on us. Sometimes he would stop speaking for days at a time if he'd had a row with my mother.

He would not only stop speaking to my mother for days on end though, but us kids too - the innocent victims caught up in it all. The atmosphere was horrendous; you could cut it with a knife. For days and days, we had to walk on eggshells - scared stiff of upsetting him in case we got the backlash.

Even today, I can't tolerate long silences if I'm in a room with other people. I have to speak or get them to speak. And if I ever have an argument with a girlfriend, I can't take the silent treatment. I have to clear the air. I will always try to make up if that's what it takes. But if I feel it has come to the point where we can no longer communicate - its time to move on. It was a particularly unhappy time of my life and choosing a parent was something I never dreamed I would ever have to do.

Carol didn't need to do this as she was nineteen at the time whereas I was still a minor. She was going out with a nice lad called Gerald (Ged), who lived only a few doors away, so she was able to escape it to a point.

I know the whole ordeal had a devastating effect on her emotionally though.

Ged saw her washing my father's car one day, and asked her out on a date. It was a fairytale romance and they've been happily married now for over thirty years.

They've got two lovely daughters (my nieces) and I'm proud to say recently, I became a great uncle. I always sort of envied my sisters life because that sort of happiness is all I've ever wanted. I could never understand why I couldn't just have the same.

The family break up was messy with lots of arguments and interference from in-laws and it was around this time, my deviant behaviour started to emerge. I was around the age of fifteen. It started with me playing truant from school.

Quite often I get asked when it all started to change for me. Well this was it. As I emotionally struggled to deal with the break up of my parents, a drastic change in my behaviour started to surface - practically overnight.

It wasn't just the fact they were separating but the way my father dealt with the situation and how his family caused so much trouble over it - although it had absolutely nothing to do with them. As well as truancy, there were several other wayward things I started to do out of character such as stealing, flying into rages, refusing to conform, rebelling against authority and shutting myself off from the outside world. It was a strange time because my dad continued living under the same roof as us for a while due to an agreement whereby they had to live separate lives in the same house. This was just soul destroying for the rest of us.

He even had his own separate food cupboard with a pad lock attached to stop us from stealing any of his food. But sometimes he forgot to lock it so I stole what I could.

Before my parents had announced their impending divorce, I had been what you may have described as a model child.

I spent most of my early teenage years locking myself in my bedroom. My bedroom became my first prison - a place where I could shut myself away for hours a day to avoid the world. I didn't need anyone else but I became such a recluse and started acting oddly - even more withdrawn, not speaking, barely leaving the house and now totally incapable of socialising.

It was also a time when it wasn't the 'norm' to be from a broken home, so I felt even more isolated. It was from this point I began to have labels attached to me from others because coming from a broken home in the 1970s was taboo. I couldn't talk to anyone about it and I didn't know anyone else who had divorced parents. I started to become angry and very bitter. My mother was now left to fend for herself where previously she'd had my father's income, albeit a pittance and an insult. Because of the lack of money available, she used to make some of our clothes, knit, darn and mend. She made do with what she had, as she could afford very little. Carol and I got 50p a week pocket money in return for household chores.

During the height of the divorce proceedings, Social Services had started to get involved. They felt that with the strain of my father still living under the same roof as us and the stress of the divorce, that my mother and I should have a short break away somewhere.

They took us to a remote farm in Barnard Castle, County Durham, where we were to live for a week in an old converted barn.

The barn was a cold stone building just inside the farm gates with steps leading up to it. Inside was a shabby settee and chair in one room and a bunk bed in another.

At night you could hear the mice or rats scratching away. There were cobwebs everywhere and yet we somehow managed to make the best of it. One of the ladies from Social Services handed my mother four pounds for the week for us both to live on. Day by day, my mother meticulously planned out what we could eat and how much we could spend. After all she'd had plenty of practice over the years living on small amounts of money she had had to beg for from my father.

The money soon ran out, so my mother decided it was time to head home a few days earlier than planned.

Eventually, my father left us to go and live on his own while seeing his new woman he'd met at work. He worked at the local sports hall as a caretaker where I used to train at the gym.

It didn't bother him how it might be making me feel seeing him flirting with her. It was heartbreaking to think that while my mother was sat at home suffering the consequences of the break up he blatantly courted his new lady friend right under my nose. My mother is the most loyal person I know and in many ways too good for this world. She never met anyone else after my father.

CHAPTER FOUR

IN NEED OF A ROLE MODEL

The transformation that started to take place in me around this time was significant because I was going through puberty and was desperate for a strong male role model in my life. I was taking more of an interest in girls whereas at school I was just a 'drop-out' kid. But now I was starting to develop a good physique and athletic prowess. My father had left, but had never been a role model anyway. There was only myself and my mother at home, so who could I speak to about girls or the changes going on inside me I didn't understand?

I couldn't talk to my mother about 'man' things. We'd never talked about things in our family anyway. It had never been encouraged to discuss things of a sensitive nature such as girls or the 'birds and the bees'.

Everything was 'hush hush'. Yet inside of me was a desperate young lad with raging hormones desperate for guidance. We never saw any sign of affection at home and I found it difficult to display this later in life until I started courting when it then became an outpouring of misguided emotion - as it was quite suffocating for those I showered with affection.

My first love who I met in York couldn't get me to hold hands in public. It took her several weeks to get me to succumb to this as I had never done it before. I know my unnatural upbringing of not seeing affection or being able to talk about things went a long way towards me developing a rather stunted and disturbed personality. My mother was always affectionate, but generally things were not talked about or displayed. I just didn't know how to behave. I was either emotionally over the top or emotionless. This was the root cause of my oppressed social skills.

When I was suffering, I didn't know how to communicate my feelings - neither did I have anyone to communicate them to. My problems and emotions then festered away inside me for many years to come.

Carol had moved in with Ged by now and I felt even more isolated. I know my mother had great concerns about my behaviour too.

I was starting to become more and more disobedient and erratic - taking advantage of the fact that there was no one around who could control me. She carried on trying to stay strong and keep me on the right track while at the same time struggling with the divorce.

Around this time, my grandfather, Harry, (my father's father) felt it would be a good idea to get more involved with the family. He did help us a lot offering advice and supporting my mother through it all. After all, he knew my father better than anyone and had despised the way he'd treated us.

It was also clear that there was huge resentment between the two of them going way back.

My father's mother had never liked my mother either and had always made it quite clear she wasn't welcome in the family. She'd always blamed her for taking her precious son away from her and just picked on her all the time. The truth was he couldn't wait to escape her overbearing clutches. She also picked on her because she spoke and acted differently - picking on her every word.

The kitchen at my grandmothers was the hub of gossip and secret whispers. You could walk in and it would go silent. It's where the world was 'put to rights' and all the malicious tongue-wagging took place. My grandfather however, was a more placid type of person. We eventually decided that he should move into the family home as he could give us back some stability. Also, he was unhappy living with my grandmother who was one of the most vicious natured women I ever met. We had a spare room and we all got on well, so he came to live with us. However, not long after, underlying problems began to surface.

For one, I would not be told what to do. I was fifteen-years-old and I had just seen the back of a domineering, controlling father. And I have to say, my grandfather's mannerisms and personality traits were exactly the same as my fathers.

This was like a red rag to a bull. It is a well-known fact that you don't really know a person until you live with them and this was a perfect example. He would lecture and try to brow beat my mother and me.

My mother would, as always, defend me to the hilt while trying to keep the peace at the same time. I could hear them always arguing about me.

I would sit at the bottom of the stairs on the other side of the door, listening to him criticising me, telling her how much of a bad son I was. I would listen to their every word, slowly going out of my mind. For it was at this time of my life I started to develop paranoia - another significant change in my personality - which then led to violent outbursts.

This often resulted in me shouting or smashing things to pieces in violent rages brought on by sheer frustration.

It was obvious that my mother had become dependent on my grandfather as he was now paying the bills and had a real hold over us. But his overbearing manner and arrogance would just 'fuel the fire' and tear my life apart.

My mother was torn as she needed all the support she could get which my grandfather provided, yet she wanted her son to be happy too. I've always felt cheated never having experienced the support and care of loving grandparents. Apart from the tormented experience I had living with my grandfather; there was never any bond or affection from my grandmother either.

On my mothers side I have heard so many things about her parents. My mother's father was a staff sergeant in the Yorkshire Regiment and a survivor of the Somme. He had also fought in the Boer war and during the Second World War worked as an air raid warden in York.

He had been stationed in Germany, then Catterick and Strensall barracks over his thirty year army career. An orphan with a horrific childhood, he had lied about his age to enlist into the army. And in 1899 at the age of fifteen went to fight in the second Boer war - preferring this to being a servant.

My grandmother was born in Camden town in London. She was a very talented pianist and a very proud woman. She was a religious, well read lady who came from a strict Victorian background. Sadly they both died when I was only one-year-old so I have no memories of them at all. Instead I only ever knew the cold, shallow side of my father's family.

My mother was worried about how withdrawn and disturbed I'd become, so she suggested I went to see a child psychologist, to which I agreed. We both went together to *St Luke's Hospital* in Middlesbrough. The psychologist agreed that my resentment towards my grandfather and his domineering presence in the house was extremely damaging and unsettling. It was mutually agreed that I should become an outpatient at their Adolescent Unit then later it was decided that I should be an inpatient which I was for three months. This was a ward for disturbed teenagers from difficult backgrounds. It seemed bizarre to most adults that a fifteen-year-old could suffer from depression. I learned very quickly that there was a lot of stigma and ignorance surrounding depression. It was very much misunderstood in those days and still is today.

There was a very strict German nurse and a husband and wife team running the ward. I was given a job in the main stores which would lead to my first step on the career ladder.

Each day I would walk from the adolescent unit across to the main stores through all the corridors where I would pass lots of adult patients on the way. And when I was delivering supplies around the hospital wards with my workmate who was - also from the adolescent unit - I'd see some very scary people.

From my child's eyes, I saw them as people who could potentially attack me any moment. But just the sight of some of them talking to themselves, the way they stared at me and their strange physical appearances, was terrifying.

It was like walking amongst the living dead. Some looked just like zombies - spaced out on tranquillisers.

During one of my weekend home visits, I bought a guitar and was trying to teach myself some chords, when by chance; my mother met new neighbours Dennis and Janet Shaw. They had three children and lived directly opposite us and had not long been in our street.

She introduced me to Dennis who was a brilliant guitarist and vocalist who had spent many years touring the pubs and clubs. He was a resident singer at the *Oak Leaf* in South Bank during his youth and a close friend of comedian Roy Chubby Brown. I immediately struck up a friendship and bond with the whole family. I became very attached to them as I was in desperate need of a family life and father figure. Each night I went across to their house to escape the miserable atmosphere at home. Dennis taught me more chords each day and how to play until eventually, I became quite competent.

At meal times, Janet would always include me with the family and it would sometimes be after eleven in the evening before I returned home.

My grandfather was always needling me that I was begging to be part of their family. It was true, but as I pointed out to him, it was only because of his and his son's failure to be good role models.

Eventually, I actually moved in and lived with the Shaw family for quite a while. Dennis became the most important male role model to me during my teenage years. He took me under his wing calling me the 'son he'd never had'. He was a tough character - a weight lifting champion with a black belt in Judo and was well respected in the community. His influence over me was paramount during my early development of masculinity.

He was everything a young male needed in a role model. He had good morals and a strong work ethic. I idolised him and he helped me more than he probably ever realised. I know he felt let down whenever I got into trouble and I felt I'd let him down too.

There's no doubt that had it not been for Dennis toughening me up, I couldn't have survived army training and prison life the way I did.

He did talk to me about the 'birds and the bees' and helped me pluck up the courage to ask a girl out on my first ever date. He explained things to me only a father and son could discuss. I let him down over and over again. But despite his endless patience giving me good advice and trying to steer me in the right direction, the damage had already been done years before. He always said he wished he had got me when I was younger. Sadly Dennis died in 2008, aged sixty-five, but I will never forget how he helped me through my mixed-up adolescence. Writing his obituary for the local press was one of the hardest things I've ever had to write.

I would still grow up with massive failings to overcome and deep seated problems, but Dennis had now given me the tools to survive.

Most importantly though, I would one day find myself giving the same advice to other young men as he had me. I had listened and I had learned. It was merely just a matter of time before I was strong enough to put it all into practice.

CHAPTER FIVE

BRING BACK
NATIONAL SERVICE!

Although my disastrous and brief army career ended after only one year, I am adamant that I managed to draw some invaluable experiences from it. And although I was dishonourably discharged and later landed myself in prison, I had learned self-discipline, self-respect and respect for authority, the importance of fitness and good manners. In the end, it was my choice to rebel against army rules and break the law, but this had no reflection on what I had learned from my time in the army. I never forgot the positive things I was taught and I was always able to call on this discipline whenever I needed it.

Ironically, it made prison easier, but the important thing, was the good things I gleaned from the army. And it would do no harm to instil this into today's youth. National Service would teach the skills I learned. I admit I started to go off the rails once I started drinking alcohol and it was the army that introduced me to it, but, my real problems were already deeply rooted.

I had officially left school in 1979 into a recession with no qualifications or job prospects whatsoever. The North was hit hard with unemployment and I could see no future staying in Middlesbrough. The best solution I felt was to join the forces. It would give me a trade and straighten me out - or so I thought. I was sixteen at the time and had been working on the Youth Opportunities Programme at ICI. This was a government scheme for helping sixteen to eighteen-year-olds into employment. I was paid £23.50 a week and was moved around the site every few weeks starting in the post room for a while, then at *Wilton Golf Course* where I got chance to drive a tractor and help maintain the grounds. I was then sent to work in the main stores. But the YOP scheme was temporary, so I set my heart on joining the RAF. I think there was something about the forces life I missed from my childhood.

Then I blew it when I got caught stealing from work. One day, one of my co-workers saw me sneaking a box of pencils I'd stolen from the stores into my locker and immediately reported me to the boss. We hadn't liked each other from day one. He had a real problem with me for some reason, so this was his way of getting one over on me. I was later called into the office and dismissed immediately. So many people believe that taking things from the workplace is acceptable, but it is in fact still a crime. It is theft after all.

I had an appointment at the Royal Air Force careers office and was really excited about the prospects of a career in the services. But my excitement was soon shattered. Already my past was about to start spoiling things for me - something that would become a regular occurrence over the rest of my life.

My medical records showed I'd been in *St Luke's Hospital* for depression which immediately put obstacles in my way. I remember the recruitment officer at Borough Road in Middlesbrough telling me I needed a doctor's note to state I was fit to join up. So I made the long bus journey to my doctor's surgery in Normanby to get this note that would give me a chance to start a new life. It would help me secure a career that would change my life forever. However, the doctor ruined any chance I had of this happening. I excitedly took the same long bus journey back to Middlesbrough with the doctor's note sealed inside an envelope. Once I was back at the careers office, I eagerly waited for the recruitment officer to read it and then tell me I could go ahead with enlisting.

My heart began to sink as I saw a puzzled expression come over his face as he read it to himself. To the surprise of us both, the doctor had written that I was unfit to join. 'Thanks doc' I thought. Thanks for ruining the only chance of something positive happening in my life.

I quickly learned that you can't let things keep you down for long though. You always need a 'plan B'. After the initial shock of being turned away, I tried to join several of the other armed services. I sat tests for the Merchant Navy and Royal Marines, but failed every one of them. Even if I had been given the chance of taking things further with the RAF, I would have failed the entrance test anyway.

I remember sitting the entrance exam for the Merchant Navy along with a few other hopefuls. Afterwards, we all sat waiting for our results. I glanced across at two of the examiners who I noticed were looking across at me while whispering to one another. I felt so sad - I knew I'd failed.

My failed schooling was now starting to make my life a misery. Still not allowing myself to be beaten though, I went to the army careers office next door to the RAF one, except this time I passed. At last, the perseverance had finally paid off. It was 1980 and I was so excited that I'd managed to achieve something. I'd also learned an invaluable lesson - never to give up.

I was seventeen-years-old, but inside I was still a child. Alcohol became a big part of army life and was the only way I could feel confident enough to socialise and join in with the others. I was accepted into the RAOC (Royal Army Ordnance Corps) after passing a three day initial selection test held at Birmingham's Sutton Coldfield when we were put through some basic fitness tests and a medical. I'd been well prepared for this as I was a keen runner and body builder, so I flew through the tests. We only had to do a few pull-ups, dips, sit-ups and a general fitness running test.

At the end of the selection weekend, we were asked to choose our preferred regiment. My choice was the Green Howards, but the recruitment officer persuaded me to join the RAOC. I wish I'd stuck to my guns and insisted on the Green Howards, as I needed the level of excitement and physical training the infantry offered.

Before joining up, I was sent a travel warrant to start my training on November 17 1980. I met a few of the lads at Camberley train station in Surrey where we all got the bus into Deepcut where Blackdown barracks was situated. This was where I was to spend the next three months doing basic training. As the bus approached I could hear the sound of gun fire and loud voices shouting orders from the parade square.

We spent our first day marching around the camp trying to keep in step. Our first stop was the barbers where a really effeminate barber shaved the sides and back of our hair. Bearing in mind this was the 1980s and a lot of the lads were into the fashion of the day, so they were devastated watching all their curls and locks fall to the ground.

Most of the haircuts looked ridiculous after the barber had sheered us because some of the lads insisted on leaving as much hair on top as possible and just having it shaved around the edges. The army rules were that anything under your hat was yours, the rest was theirs. It was easier just to get the whole lot shaved off. In those days having a shaved head meant you were either a skinhead or squaddie (soldier). We were then marched to the clothing store known as the Quartermasters where we walked along the front of a long bench where our new uniforms, kit and bedding items were hurled at us until they were piled up so high, we couldn't see over the top.

Marching everywhere in ranks of three, dressed in all the fashions and bright colours of the 1980s, must have been a sight to see. One lad called 'Punky' turned up wearing torn jeans with chains, safety pins and piercings through various body parts. We were expected to know our regimental numbers off-by-heart now because we'd already been given a letter at the army careers office with them on, once we'd sworn the oath.

I remember swearing my oath upstairs in the army careers office to a rather eccentric major. He held a bible in one hand while reading out passages of the oath that I had to repeat back. During this very important part of enlisting, one of his lenses fell from his spectacles landing on his desk. I burst out laughing and then struggled on repeating the oath while desperately trying to stifle my giggling.

We were then taken to the Borneo Platoon block where we were given our bed spaces. There were several other platoons situated in identical buildings nearby and we were always encouraged to compete against one another in competitions, sports and training.

Now it was over to the cookhouse which was a huge dining hall and so busy. It was a daunting sort of experience at first with hundreds of people everywhere. The queues were enormous with lines of hungry men from various regiments and women from the *Women's Royal Army Corps*. One lone soldier in the dinner queue stood out from the crowd to me. I noticed his SAS uniform straight away, firstly from the regiment's epilates and then the familiar blue stable belt. I wanted to belong to the SAS regiment as I had read books about them at home and was in awe of their assault on the Iranian Embassy that year.

There was a trolley in the cookhouse where you scraped your plates and piled them up. Sometimes, if the staff were over busy, the pile got so high it would then come crashing to the floor. When it was me who put that final plate on top causing it to topple, I used to get out fast so they wouldn't see that it was me who had sent them all smashing to the ground.

There was always the sound of music coming from speakers situated around the cookhouse. I recall Neil Diamond's new release, *Love on the rocks* filling the air with such poignancy. Not long after breakfast, we'd be inspected outside the platoon block and then told to get changed into our PT kits for fitness training. Our kit consisted of long blue shorts, tee-shirts and black plimsolls if we were training in the gym.

If we were running, we wore khaki lightweight trousers, tee-shirts and boots. A few of us got stitches during the early morning runs which wasn't surprising, seeing as we'd only eaten breakfast about an hour before. But missing breakfast is an offence in the army. If you collapse while on the parade square and it's discovered you missed breakfast, you can be charged, although this is never done. It's one of those rules that remains in existence but not taken seriously.

Sometimes we'd run in full combat gear which consisted of heavy camouflaged jackets and trousers, boots, ammunition pouches and carrying a 9lb SLR (self loading rifle). I remember during one run, one of the lads smashing head-first into a lamppost when a young lady caught his eye from the roadside. We ran along the roads led by a PTI (Physical Training Instructor). There'd be one at the front and one at the rear wearing aluminous vests watching and directing traffic. Some of our PTIs were a breed of their own - very over confident, full of themselves and very much full of their own importance. Years later I met one of them again in Durham prison.

The twelve weeks basic training was great. I was always at the front of the ranks when we were out running and first at everything else too. And thanks to Dennis Shaw teaching me some self defence techniques back home, I knew some Aikido moves too which we did as part of our 'battle' PT lessons. Later in life I would gain a black belt in Aikido. One of our PTIs, Corporal Barley who was from Wales, had a real evil streak.

He and some of his sidekicks took us all for our swimming test to the officer training school at Sandhurst one Saturday morning. I was a non swimmer, so I welcomed the lessons. But to my horror, we weren't there for a day out at the swimming baths. We all lined up at the edge of the pool while one of the junior ranks, Lance Corporal Hawkings, demonstrated how easy it was to stay afloat by filling your lungs with air. Then Cpl. Barlcy told all the non swimmers to stand at the twelve foot end of the pool. Then he ordered us all to jump in and tread water for three minutes on his command.

Totally petrified, we followed his orders and all jumped in. After all, we were starting to become brain washed by now, so we didn't question, we just did what we were ordered to do. As soon as we hit the water, we all started panicking as we fought to stay afloat, sinking and swallowing large gulps of water - frantically struggling not to drown. I could feel myself sinking lower and lower, desperately struggling to stay afloat. Then me and another lad, who was also panicking, decided to just swim to the side of the pool, get out of the water and to hell with orders. One of the junior ranks - a lance corporal - who thought he was incredibly tough and God's gift was screaming at us to jump back in. I just ignored him, he was an idiot. Cpl. Barley revealed to us later that in one of the last batches of recruits he took to the pool, one of the non swimmers drowned 'because he wouldn't stay still' he said. What a shame he hadn't disobeyed his orders like I had and got out of the pool.

We were barracked in (confined to camp) most nights, but I didn't drink then, so it didn't bother me. Then exactly three weeks into training, shocking news came over the radio announcing that John Lennon had been assassinated. One of my all time favourite songs I was always playing at the time, (*Just like*) *Starting Over,* was released only weeks before his death.

The platoon corporal in charge of us, Corporal Cooper, was like a *Jekyll and Hyde* character. He'd pay random visits to the block at all times of the night 'worse for wear' and get us to do change parades just for the hell of it. I know it was all part of the training, but he definitely had a screw loose.

Change parades would start with us all being ordered to stand outside our block in ranks of three. We'd then be ordered to get changed into particular clothing items and be back outside in the fastest time possible. The junior ranks would be pushing us down the stairs and screaming at us. Thinking of it now, makes me giggle, but at the time I was scared stiff. I was more nervous of things than most who just took things in their stride.

One night we were told to get changed into full combats, helmets, wearing our respirators (gas masks) and be back downstairs as fast as possible carrying our mattresses on our shoulders. Once we were all congregated back outside in three ranks, we were then taken for a run around the camp and across the parade square. What a sight we must have been. Without the corporal noticing, I unscrewed the canister from my respirator so I could take in large gulps of fresh air. Our respirators were used for nuclear biological and chemical (NBC) warfare training.

This included entering a gas chamber where we were taken through a survival drill consisting of several small tests. I'd been dreading what awaited us as we were taken across to the sinister looking brick building which had no windows - just a door.

We were all kitted out in our NBC suits (noddy suits) with our respirators in pouches. An NBC suit consisted of a smock with hood and trousers which was worn over the uniform with the webbing on the outside and it was not the most comfortable thing to wear. There was a contraption in the centre of the chamber where a CS gas canister was ignited quickly filling the air with thick smoke.

The drill consisted of us removing our respirators - just enough to eat a biscuit and drink some water and replace them again. Unfortunately for me, when I replaced my respirator, the seal wasn't covering my face properly, so gas leaked though the sides choking me.

At the end of the drill, we were all met at the door one at a time by Cpl. Cooper where we had to remove our respirators completely and then answer a few questions such as number, rank and name. It was all to get us used to the gas, the smell and the burning sensation of it.

By the time it was my turn to leave, my eyes were streaming and my face felt as though it was on fire, not to mention the uncontrollable coughing fit I had. One of the NCOs said, 'Let him out, he's had enough.' The next time I got a taste of CS gas like that was many years later when

I was sprayed by several police officers I was wrestling with. The dormitories housed twelve recruits and our daily routine began with roll call at 5.30am where we would first of all make a bed pack which consisted of one blanket on top of a sheet, on top of a blanket, with a blanket wrapped around them, then our pillows placed on top. We left one sheet on the bed with the top cover folded half way down.

Our metal mess tins, which were what we ate our food from when we were out in the field on exercise, had to be immaculate. Boots had to be 'bulled' (spit and polished with a rag) with layers and layers of polish, soaked overnight, and then buffed the next day.

One of our routines was to take turns buffing the floor, the buffer being a heavy metal attachment on the end of a heavy broom handle. We all learned how to iron too which we did each night ready for the next morning as well as polishing the bathroom basins, baths and taps.

One of our main jobs right at the start of training was to burn our boots. In those days, we were issued with two pairs of boots. Both had pimples down and around the sides. One pair was used for everyday use so we only had to 'bull' the toe cap. The other pair was our 'best boots' and had to have an overall shine.

Therefore to get this shine, we had to spend one night with lighted candles and a spoon burning off all these pimples until the entire boot was smooth. You heated the back of the spoon and then pushed it across the boot melting the pimples off. It was a lengthy and boring process, but we all sat around having a good 'crack' while doing it. I flew through basic training with flying colours achieving the highest fitness assessment score of 178 which was calculated from how many push-ups we could do, how many sit-ups we could do and so on. I remember doing almost one hundred inclined sit ups on a wooden bench which were counted out by one of my mates, at which point, Cpl. Barley intervened and told me to stop and to stand to attention. He said, 'Well done Honeywell.' That was one of the biggest boosts I had ever had, but not as much as when he later announced all the individual scores in the changing room. Deliberately missing my name out, he shouted, 'Has anyone's name not been read out?' I raised my arm.

'Stand up Honeywell'! he said. He read out my score of 178 as being the highest ever achieved in the platoon for which I received a rapturous applause and the bumps.

It was so strange how far I had come along with physical fitness since my school days. Only two years earlier, I was so terrified taking part in any kind of sports or PT activities; I would deliberately leave my kit at home knowing I would be slippered. Yet all that changed after one teacher praised me up. I now wonder - had this happened much earlier in my childhood, how different my school years could have been. A confident team player? Runner? Confident boy? Quite possibly.

The NAAFI (Navy, Army and Air Force Institutes), was the local shop and bar on the camp. Some weekends other regiments would visit and whenever the Parachute Regiment turned up, there was always trouble. We had plastic beer glasses, the sort of thing which we tend to associate with today's culture, yet this was 1981. When we were given guard duty, we would wear our combats and sleep over in the guardroom through the night taking turns with our 'stag' duty. I hated being woken up every four hours to go and patrol around the camp carrying pick-axe handles. Some drunk would always try and test you on their way back from the pub. Once Borneo platoon reached the end of the twelve weeks basic training, it was celebrated with a passing out parade. Families and friends were invited to watch us all proudly marching in our number twos (best uniforms). It was a proud, emotional day. My mother came with friends and Dennis and Janet Shaw came along with their kids.

We all got weekend leave passes after which we returned to take up our trade training as supply specialists (storemen/women).

The sergeant running the course referred to himself as God, and I took an instant dislike to him.

There was another sergeant who was assisting him who came from Middlesbrough. He was nice man, but showed me up one day pointing out something I got wrong to the whole class which brought back bad school memories. The truth is I hated it all. When I was running around during basic training, I loved every minute of it; even if I was scared at times of some of the MTIs (military training instructors). But it suited me.

One weekend, I went on a little jaunt to London where I soaked up the delights of Soho and several pubs elsewhere. I was late getting back on Monday morning after sleeping rough at a train station in London. The sergeant, who thought he was God, disliked me almost as much as I disliked him and I didn't try to hide it.

This was a period of my life when my attitudes started to change towards authority figures who thought they were God. At end of the three week trade training, when he announced we'd all passed our exams, he deliberately pointed out to the whole class that I had only got through by the skin of my teeth. Some were emotional and hugging one another after passing. I looked on detached from the rest of them and completely uncaring about any of it. I was relieved it had ended, but I had no emotion whatsoever, except a sudden realisation that I was in the wrong regiment. The past several weeks of trade training under an egotistical sergeant and his side kick increased my hatred for classrooms and exams even more. Being a Supply Specialist wasn't the most exciting job, so I spent several months trying to transfer to the Infantry. I wasn't supported at all with my application; instead I was just met with sniggers and petty comments by bigoted admin workers. They eventually refused to take my application any further forward. It was at that point, I lost all interest in the RAOC, the army and any desire to conform.

Soon after completing the first part of our trade training, we were then sent to RAF Leconfield near Beverley - about ten miles from Hull. Here we were to do the second part of our trade training which was to gain our HGV (heavy goods vehicle) licence. This was an expected part of our Supply Specialist role.

It was an excellent opportunity. They took you through learning to drive a car if you couldn't already drive, to driving a *Land Rover,* then to HGV level when you could drive large *Bedford* army trucks. I was still teetotal so I basically felt like an outcast to a point. This was a real bonus during basic training because I had the upper-hand always being fitter than the rest. But now I was part of a different culture - a drinking culture.

Each morning, we had roll call in an aircraft hanger before going off to our driving lessons. Id been in many of these places as a child. We were all designated a driving instructor. Mine was a rather tough looking sergeant who was towards the latter end of his army service. With our instructors, we then went through a daily drill of checking tyre pressures, checking the engine and so on. All this is beyond me now. I wouldn't have a clue. For some reason, I just couldn't see it through. I didn't like my instructor's manner either. He was gruff and arrogant. But he wasn't the worst I'd met. I was so nervous driving; I stalled the car at a major roundabout in Doncaster one day. It was so busy and it freaked me out.

A few days later, after roll call, I went into the office and confessed that I should be wearing glasses but didn't have any. This was my way of getting out of it. I was then RTU'd (returned to unit). But it was what I had wanted. It would also be yet another lifelong regret. Being a non-driver has caused me so many difficulties over the years. Not long after, we were given our postings.

That was when things went rapidly downhill for me. I was posted to 10 Ordnance Support Battalion just outside a small town in Wiltshire called Devizes. Nowadays, I'd be fascinated by this village as it's purported to be one of the most haunted towns in the UK, but when I was eighteen, I was bored senseless with the place. I didn't like the daily nine to five work routine in the stores, or where I was posted. Neither did I like the regiment. But I'd get a chance to change this six years later when I was accepted for selection into the Special Air Service's (Territorial Army).

Once I had transferred to Devises, I soon started drinking and smoking heavily. It was such a tedious place where drinking was the order of the day. We had money, local girls on tap, and we made the most of it. But this would be the downfall of my army career and the start of my reckless lifestyle for many years to come.

Alcohol got the better of me so much that I got to the stage of even missing the morning roll call and getting someone to answer to my name. I had gone from being a teetotal, non smoking super fit soldier during basic training, with a promising army career ahead of me, to a drunken, chain smoking individual without a care in the world for anyone and rebellious against authority.

All my wages went on beer and fags. These were things I'd never done before, but I wanted to fit in and felt as though drinking would help me be 'one of the lads'. It was my alcohol consumption that would become my nemesis. Before joining the army, I was teetotal and for someone who is prone to depression, consuming alcohol was the worst thing I could do. It led to me going AWOL (absent without leave) which I always did while under the influence.

One night I took a taxi all the way from Devizes to my home in Eston. As the months passed, I became increasingly home-sick and bored to death. I started going AWOL on a regular basis, where I would go back home to Middlesbrough, then two or three days later, return to barracks thinking I could carry on where I left off. Each time, I would be hauled in front of the commanding officer to be given my punishment. During the days leading up to this I would be placed under 'close arrest' which basically meant I was confined to barracks. When my time came to be dealt with, I'd be anxiously waiting outside the C.O.s office standing in the middle of two escorts.

The door would suddenly burst open and a warrant officer would shout, 'Quick march!' You marched in at a faster-than-normal pace into the office around the front of the desk where the C.O. was sitting to our left, and came to attention. Then you would wait for the order - 'Left turn!' so you were facing the C.O. One day I turned right by mistake so my back was facing the C.O. He then had to shout 'Left turn' twice until I was facing him.

I could slightly see out the corner of my eye the lance corporal to my right desperately trying to stop laughing. I could see his shoulders going up and down and could hear him trying to control his giggling. I was given a fine and told to carry on with my duties.

It seemed like a long time in that office, but we had a good laugh about it afterwards. This didn't stop me going AWOL though and after going absent again, I was given my first ever taste of prison in the army glasshouse (detention) which was a short sharp shock that would shock me to the core. The glasshouse is no picnic. The difference between a military prison and a civilian prison is that you can be locked up in a military prison for offences that breach military rules, but are not necessarily criminal offences.

Offences in the army can include going AWOL, drunk and disorderly, and anything that they think warrants a stint in jail. I once saw a recruit being swiftly marched to the guardroom with a mattress on his shoulder because he had love bites all over his neck. At least if I'd been done for this, I would have felt it had been worth it. The difference is of course, once you've done your sentence, you can return to normal duties and 'soldier on' as they say, whereas in 'civvy' street, you will struggle to live a normal life after being convicted.

A term in the glasshouse was always said to make you a better soldier because of the brutal regime. Although Colchester is the main glasshouse in the military, each camp has their own guardroom with cells and some are run like Colchester. Military prison is knick-named the glasshouse because everything inside is polished and buffed like glass so you can see your face in it.

The first experience of seeing inside a military prison cell was when I was ten-years-old when we lived at RAF Leeming. My father took me to the guardroom one day where he showed me a small, bare, cold room which had a solid wooden bench for a bed and at the head of the bench was one folded grey blanket. The barred window was so high up that anyone who had to spend time in there would never be able to reach to see out. It served no purpose other than to allow a glimmer of light through.

The floor was like glass, gleaming from the reflection of the light coming through the bars. There was a hatch on the door which was used to pass food to prisoners. I remember feeling shocked at how severe it all looked and was trying to imagine how terrible it must be for anyone to have to spend a night in this grim place. Little did I know that eight years later I would be locked inside one myself.

My second experience as an observer was when I was stationed at Blackdown Barracks. I kept seeing this young soldier being marched around everywhere at a mad pace while being screamed at by the provost sergeant following behind him. The prisoner had his hair shaved and was stripped of all identity.

He wasn't wearing his beret or any jacket; he just had his khaki shirt, lightweights and boots without laces. But what really caught my eye, was that outside the front of the guardroom stood an empty coffin leaning against the wall. When I asked about it, I was told it was because the prisoner had attempted suicide.

He was being 'beasted' around like an animal because he was depressed enough to make an attempt on his own life. And the coffin was to make him think twice about doing it again. Provost staff (regimental police) were a joke really. They took themselves far too seriously and always dressed to impress.

Their hat peaks and boots shone like glass. If the peak of their hats weren't slashed, they did it themselves to make themselves look meaner. A slashed peak is where they cut the lining of the hat and pushed the peak further in so it fits low over the bridge of their nose. If anyone else did this, they were charged for damaging military property.

Well it was now my turn to be 'beasted' and I was soon to get the shock of my life.

CHAPTER SIX

THE 'GLASSHOUSE'

The thing that landed me in the glasshouse first time around was when I deserted while away on exercise in Denmark. I was later told that if you do a runner from camp, it's AWOL, but if you're away on exercise it's classed as desertion. And apparently you can still be shot for it, but I knew that wasn't going to happen.

En route to Denmark, we all stayed over at Brize-Norton ready to fly out the next morning. On the journey in the *Hercules*, I took a supply of beer by filling my ammunition pouches with cans of lager. I noticed there were some sick bags for anyone who felt the need to vomit but I wasn't going to drink on the plane so I wouldn't need one. They were exactly like the ones my father used to bring home for my travel sickness when I was a kid. I was excited to be going abroad for the first time, we had all been given our wages in Danish Krone and I intended to make the most of it.

Once we arrived, the thing that struck me most was how clean all the roads and streets were everywhere. At the barracks where we were to stay for the next six weeks, I noticed the native soldiers were a lot less formal than we were. They all had shoulder length hair and walked around playing with yo-yos.

We were barracked-in most nights and worked most of the day, and then spent what was left of the evenings watching television and generally being even more bored to tears than back at our base in England. We did get some time away though. On our first night we all headed to Copenhagen for drinks and a traditional visit to the red-light district. I lost my virginity that night which cost me 200 Krone for half an hour. I was ushered into this chic looking boudoir by a stunning blonde Danish lady.

After that night, we were all barracked in again night after night, until I'd had enough. So one day I told the corporal in charge that I had to go to the bank to draw some cash out.

I was in fact heading for the train station and then for Copenhagen where I went on the run for a week. I spent my days drinking in bars and sleeping rough. Looking back I have no idea why I wanted to put myself through that kind of ordeal. I even got a job for a time working as a washer-up at the capital's train station restaurant.

But one of the waitresses told the manager I was a deserter who then fired me. I don't know why I told her I was a deserter. I suppose I thought it would impress her. After a week, the money ran out and I was exhausted, hungry and missing life's little luxuries, so I turned myself in to the Danish Police who then escorted me to the British Embassy.

At the Embassy, I was met by a real English gentleman who was obviously in charge. And I think was either an army officer or a former one. He ushered me into a huge posh office which had leather chairs and polished tables. We talked for a while, when he suddenly said, 'Have you got any cigarettes?' while at the same time taking a packet of *John Players* from his pocket and handing me the few he had left. I thought it was a nice gesture. I think he probably realised I had lived like a tramp during my stint on the run and took pity on me. I also noticed on the table in front of me a tall plastic container full of complimentary cigarettes for visitors. When he had to leave the office for a moment to ring the army provost crew to come and collect me, I helped myself to a handful of them, quickly stuffing them in my jacket pocket. When the provost crew turned up, they all strutted in led by the ever arrogant Sergeant Major Malone who was an imposing individual who liked to try and intimidate people with his physical size and loud mouth.

I was quite embarrassed though when the motley crew ordered me to turn out my pockets. There I was taking out a handful of the cigarettes I'd just helped myself to while the Embassy gent was out of the room. I looked over to him but he didn't even 'bat an eyelid', - a true gent I thought, unlike the rabble who I had to travel back to camp with. I may have been a law breaker and a pain over the years, but I have always been as polite and courteous as I can and never acted like a Neanderthal, unlike a lot I have had the misfortunate to spend time with.

The motley crew took me back to camp where I was met with hostility and contempt from others who didn't even know me or were even in the same regiment. It's always easy to target a vulnerable individual when you're amongst a group of other like-minded people. But they always fail to understand that anyone can one day find themselves on the wrong side of the law.

However, I hadn't broken the law, I had broken army rules. When you're under arrest in the army, just like the soldier I saw at Blackdown, you're marched everywhere at a ridiculously fast pace and stripped of all identity. You're not allowed to wear your hat or have laces in your boots. You're not allowed to associate or even speak to your comrades, because you've supposedly disgraced the regiment. I remember standing outside the C.O.s office awaiting to hear my fate for the rest of my time in Denmark when I heard the song *One Day In Your Life* by

Michael Jackson playing on someone's radio and thinking how much I liked the dulcet sound of this ballad.

An officer then escorted me to what was to be my place of work for the next few days. It was a large field where they had been serving meals to the troops. There were hundreds of large dirty pots, pans and kitchen utensils scattered around, cigarette butts everywhere and a general mess. It's ironic that this would become my work in civilian life when I was released from prison in 1985 which I will come to later.

Nearby, there were dormitories where I could see other squaddies milling around inside suffering the boredom that had driven me to this. I had been given ROPs (restriction of privileges) and put to work as a general 'dogs-body' washing and sweeping-up and running errands. This sort of punishment used to be called jankers. Whenever they got the opportunity, the other squaddies would try to humiliate me by throwing their fag butts on the floor outside their windows for me to sweep up, or by making childish remarks.

A few days later I was flown back to Gatwick airport on a *Hercules*. Apart from the pilot, there was only myself and a young lady from the WRACs on the entire plane. Before boarding the plane, Malone passed my files to her asking if she would look after them during the flight until we arrived at Gatwick where I was to be met by the regiment's duty provost. She looked decidedly petrified. Once I was back on UK soil, I was arrested and taken back to Devizes camp and straight to the guardroom which was just a small wooden hut, and immediately locked up. I sat most of the night planning my escape which would've been quite easy. I was allowed to come and go to the toilet where there were windows with no bars on them. I could've easily climbed through and slid down the side of the wall. I was then going to crawl underneath the guardroom which was raised on stilts, and sneak away. But in the end I decided to just accept my fate instead as I always did whenever I was in trouble with the law. I would always accept my punishment. Never did I have a problem with the police, lawyers or prison officers.

I never took the view that I was the victim and that everyone else was to blame as a lot of offenders do. Back at camp the next morning, I was quickly marched in front of the commanding officer flanked by two lance corporals either side of me. We all stood to attention until instructed to stand at ease. Lieutenant Colonel Champion read out my name and number, '24598031, Private Honeywell?' 'Yes Sir'! I replied. He then added, 'You've been charged with going absent without leave.'

After all the formalities were over, he gave me twenty-seven days' detention and ordered me to 'soldier on' once I was released. To 'soldier on' meant that once you had paid your just desserts, you could return to normal duties. What a shame the civilian criminal justice system and society can't allow ex-offenders to do this.

I was then taken by *Land Rover* on what seemed like an eternity to Warminster, escorted by Sergeant Mac, an ex paratrooper who I'd always admired and befriended. We used to go running together every day and now he was escorting me to jail which I knew he didn't like doing. He was real old school with a huge handle-bar moustache. He had great spirit and toughness. Entering the gates of the *Warminster School of Infantry* camp was quite daunting. Sgt Mac turned to me and said, 'Just get your head down and take your punishment Honeywell, then come out and start again.' I could feel the nervousness inside me increasing as the *Land Rover* neared the guardroom where a Scots guard sergeant stood waiting by the entrance clutching a pace stick. I was escorted through to the guardroom which had a desk to the left where one of the jailers was sat.

The place reeked of polish and fear. On the other side of the room was a large window through which I could see a large room with three beds in a row. The floor was immaculately polished and gleamed from the reflection of the sun that squeezed through a skylight.

I was told to stand to attention at one the end of the desk while all the formalities were discussed with Sgt. Mac, but I really had no idea what awaited me. The guards who we always had to refer to as 'staff' were garrison police, a feared arm of the military with a reputation for brutality. There was the Scottish sergeant who met us at the entrance and who happened to be a real gent actually. Then there was a Brummy lance corporal from the Irish Guards who was a decent enough bloke and hadn't time for all the army bull-shit.

There was a Liverpudlian corporal who I liked most of all because he didn't throw his weight around. He was so laid back; he was more like one of us. But then there was a psycho Black Watch corporal called Smudge Smith who I despised. He had real personal issues that he took out on us. Then there was a short corporal with a real case of 'Napoleon syndrome' who basically tried to use his loud voice to scare people because he had no presence at all.

While I was standing to attention waiting to be processed - just for a split second - he caught a glance from me at which point he ran over to me screaming, 'Are you looking at me'?

We were almost nose to nose - at least we would have been had he been tall enough. He screamed at me, 'You listen to me'! 'When I say go, you left turn, run through the back, get in your cell, and slam the door shut. 'Do you understand'!!? he screamed.

I nodded, and knew from that moment on, this was going to be hell. I knew then it was going to be a long twenty-seven days from that moment on. I was dreading what lay ahead. 'Go'! he screamed, making me almost jump out of my skin. I spun to the left, slamming my right heel into the ground bringing myself to attention.

As fast as I could, I quickly ran through the corridor behind me and into a cell situated at the far right and slammed the door behind me - a sound that I would become accustomed to over the years. My cell which was situated in a corner at the rear of the building was near some showers and looked just like the cell my father once showed me when I was a ten-year-old boy.

It had the same heavy metal door with a hatch to pass food through, but as we ate our meals at the cookhouse, it was never used for this purpose. The walls were bright red and the cell floor was also a gleaming dark red which I'm sure had been deliberately painted that colour to make us go insane. However, we didn't spend that much time in our cells, because we were always running, marching or cleaning the guardroom.

Each morning we were up at 5.00am ready to start the day with an early morning run through the nearby woods carrying a huge log on our shoulders, followed by a cold shower. There was another prisoner who was staying in that large room I'd noticed on the way in. The rest of the day we then spent polishing and cleaning the guardroom and getting our kit ready for the next mornings' inspection.

The guards would sometimes get us to do random things such as marching us up and down and around the camp. The only laugh we ever got which only lasted for a short while was with a large-built corporal from the Coldstream Guards who was temporarily brought in. He used to make us burst out laughing whenever he shouted at us. This gave us some sort of relief and helped us get through because he saw the funny side of it too.

Every morning the duty officer for that day would strut in to inspect us, our beds and kit which was all neatly laid out on top. Each night, we had to polish the peak of our hats which sat on top of our bed blocks just like we had made in basic training. Except in here they had to measure exactly nine inches by nine inches. And if it was slightly skewiff, it would be hurled to the floor.

Our best boots and shoes which we spent hours polishing until they were gleaming were carefully laid out along the sides of the bed. Down the centre of the bed were our shirts and trousers also folded and pressed to exact measurements. Then situated at the bottom, was our toothpaste tube, soap and cutlery positioned in a uniformed manner. We scrubbed the paint off our toothpaste tubes and shoe polish tins until they were silver. If the duty officer was one of those who had a point to prove, he would bring a ruler to measure our folded up shirts and blankets. It was pathetic really. On my first day, the shouting and screaming got to me and I don't mind admitting, I cried.

But I had started to accept that breaking rules came at a price and taking punishment was all part of it. We were allowed two cigarettes a day which we smoked while standing to attention. Each day was spent humiliating me in one way or another which exceeded punishment. Smudge Smith grabbed me by the throat one morning pushing me against the cell wall while squeezing my windpipe because I'd got up too early. I had already made my bed block, and had my kit all laid out before they had chance to even wake me up and he didn't like it. He would do something like this then shortly afterwards call me through to the office and offer me one of his cigarettes.

I always wished I had met some of the guards after my release. They always forget that time stands still for no man and one day most prisoners do get released. Some of the guards were scum of the earth and not interested in doing a good job.

They were just there to vent their pathetic personal issues on vulnerable prisoners. I was supposed to be the one who had disgraced the army, but at least I had never been a bully or preyed on the weak.

One of them explained to me that prisoners who they knew came from broken homes were easier to crack. My sentence finally ended and I was collected by one of the drivers and taken back to Devizes. It wasn't long before I was getting into debt, and borrowing money from everyone.

Every penny I earned was going on beer and fags so I borrowed more and more to feed my new addictions. Every night I went out on the town around the local pubs drinking myself into a stupor because there was just nothing else to do on camp. The boredom was too much, so I just drank myself into oblivion every night.

Because of my latest experiences in the glasshouse, they decided to put my newly learned talents to good use and offered me a job working as a regimental policeman. This was an easy number and it was something that suited me. I had always wanted to be a policeman when I was a young boy and throughout my teens too. The only thing that prevented me from joining the police was that I had no qualifications at the time. If I had, I most certainly would have joined the police force. This seems so bizarre to me now with all that's happened since and probably quite alarming to most people who know me too. I remember having an interview with an inspector at York police station in 1983 when I was told I needed five 'O' levels, but I knew getting these was beyond my capabilities.

That year, I ended up on the opposite side of the law and back at York police station on criminal charges and at the beginning of a journey that would give me massive regrets to this day. Back to being a regimental policeman though. We all had to do a stint guarding the gate, stopping cars and doing random checks on vehicles as they entered the camp.

Some wouldn't stop so I would always make a note of the registration number and report them. Jim, was in charge of me - a former police officer and a fearless man of large stature who I really enjoyed working with. I even learned how to direct traffic from him one day when the army held a gala day. He wasn't liked by many others though because he rubbed people up the wrong way. This was a period where I seemed to be settling down, but then the debt started getting worse and I began acting more and more erratic.

The next time I went AWOL, was the last time. It was only a few weeks since my last detention and before my feet even touched the ground, I was back in the glasshouse for another fourteen days going through all the same routine as before. My second stint in the glasshouse wasn't as bad as the first time. It was as though they had realised I was just a lost cause and that no matter how much they bawled and shouted at me, I was going home anyway. One day while I was polishing the floor, all of a sudden the door burst open and in marched Jim, followed by Sgt Mac, barking, 'Left-Right, Left-Right, Left-Right.

I couldn't believe my eyes seeing Jim carrying a suitcase with his single lance corporal stripe hanging from his sweater where it had been ripped off. I can't recall what had led to this, but I do remember that he never succumbed to the guards' bully tactics. Smudger, the guard, had tried to get me to have a word with him to get him to 'toe the line'.

They had done this with the prisoner I'd spent my time with during my twenty-seven days who threatened to kick my head in if I didn't 'screw the bob'. If only I'd had Jim's strength of character, I kept thinking.

Years later while I was in prison doing my five-year stretch, I saw Jim on *Countdown* television quiz programme.

The army had now had enough of me messing about, so they 'drummed' me out after just one year and seventeen days. It would become one of the biggest regrets of my life, but didn't stop me doing foolish things throughout my life. I still believe that had the RAOC allowed me to transfer to an infantry regiment when I asked them, I would have stayed in the army. The RAOC hated me but I hated them even more.

CHAPTER SEVEN

FIRST OFFENCE

After I left the army, I felt that society owed me and it was all society's fault that I was failing in everything I did. I had a huge chip on my shoulder and every intention of wreaking havoc. I was nineteen-years-old and had just started carrying knives. Although I have pinpointed when my early behaviour began to change, why exactly I transformed from being a timid, quiet, shy - although disturbed boy, into a persistent, violent, knife carrying offender, is more complex.

I may have stolen and been fired from my job for it and I know I'd screwed up my army career. But I wasn't a violent thug. So where did that come from? Sometimes I struggle to answer this myself, but I can clearly see, there were worrying behavioural changes during my early teens. However, it was after becoming a heavy drinker I started committing serious, violent offences fuelled by 'Dutch courage'.

This happened almost straight after being kicked out of the army. Until then the only things I'd done under the influence was going AWOL. I left the army much tougher and more confident. And because I had done some time in a military prison, I thought I was a bit of a 'tough guy'.

Part of the reason I was a knife carrier, was the same reason why today's youths carry knives. It was because a big part of me felt I needed to be in control and respected - yet at the same time - out of fear - felt the need to protect myself from being attacked by gangs. Some young men feel that carrying a weapon makes them a man, powerful and in control as I did. For most of my young life, I carried weapons - usually knives and sometimes more than one because they made me feel I was in charge and in control of all other aspects of my life that I had no control over.

When young men carry weapons, they can be their gangster role models like Ronnie Kray or Al Capone. This was a huge part of my transition from bad boy to violent thug. I felt that by aspiring to them, I would gain respect out of fear. And one day I would seek out those who had made my life a misery in the past and make them pay.

My admiration for gangsters started to develop when I began reading books about famous criminals and the MAFIA. I was inspired by a book I'd read about the Kray twins, called, *Profession of violence: The rise and fall of the Kray Twins*.

I saw them as Robin Hoods of their day - people who were well respected and should be aspired to. I connected straight away with their rebellion against the army and their stint in the glasshouse. I connected to the fact they saw the provost staff as a total joke, but respected war heroes and gentlemen officers.

I started corresponding with them. I received a reply shortly after my first letter from both Reg and Ron. I got a real 'buzz' from this. I used to watch gangster films and documentaries all the time. And I remember being glued to the television watching a series called, *Gangster Chronicles* which was a history of 'organised crime' in 1920's and 30's America.

It was their style, and fearsome reputations and their defiance towards authority that inspired me. I decided I was going to teach people lessons in respect whenever someone tried to belittle me. My first offence was a robbery on a shop near York where I used a knife to threaten a shop-keeper which I will expand on further in the chapter. The second offence was 'wounding with intent to cause grievous bodily harm' in Darlington where someone was stabbed - not by me - but with my knife. Even though it wasn't me who actually made the blow, it belonged to me and was in my possession just before it happened which resulted in a serious crime being committed.

Another night an altercation took place at a house party between me and someone who tried to take my head off with a sword. He missed and I managed to punch him busting his nose. Yet despite having just served thirty months in jail for knife crimes, I pulled out a knife which I'm sure I would have used had he pushed his luck.

The next time I used a knife, I left someone bleeding to death in the middle of a pub. Even now I can't comprehend what planet I was on at that time and still find it difficult to talk about. But though I had always been in possession of knives - it was that last incident when reality hit me like a sledgehammer of just how serious things had become.

It started to hit me that this man could have died. How many lives could that have ruined?

What a thoughtless act! This message was even further rammed home to me while spending time with life-sentence prisoners over the next two years.

Most of them had committed the exact same act of mindless violence as I had, but they had not been so lucky. I was released after two-and-a-half-years, whereas most of them had already spent an average of fifteen years inside. They all had the same thing in common in that as well as ruining their own lives; many other lives had also been ruined forever. Some had missed out on their children growing up and their marriages had ended.

People always say, if you carry a weapon then you are obviously prepared to use it and I have to say I agree with this. Several of my mates from my hometown who were real hard men were disgusted at me for carrying a knife. They were capable of using their fists to settle scores which just shows how attitudes have changed so much. Some of those men have since been murdered by knife and sword wielding individuals.

One of my lifelong friends called Peter Hoe was victim of a knife attack. He told me he wasn't impressed by what I did. We remained friends throughout our youth and adult years. He was such a polite man. Every time I met him, he'd buy me a drink and we'd reminisce about the past. He didn't really like bringing things up from the past actually. He once told me I was old school which was quite a compliment. But the fact he always had a lot of time for me was an even greater compliment. So many old friends have had their lives in such tragic circumstances.

Another was Liverpool gangster, chief lieutenant, Johnny Phillips who I met in Durham jail. He was gunned down in the 1990s. I met several gangsters from Liverpool in prison. Prison's a breeding ground for villainy. But I had no time for those who threw their weight around.

It may not be anything new and perhaps the media is hyping it up a bit - but the fact that there is still a problem, demonstrates that the country still hasn't managed to get to grips with the problem of knife crime - generation after generation.

After being kicked out of the army in 1981, I had returned to Teesside where nothing had changed. There was still high unemployment figures and a lot of men out of work who had always thought they had jobs for life. The sight of men covered in black dirt walking through the streets after a hard shift at work was becoming a less familiar sight. I'd now blown my army career and was back in Middlesbrough with my tail between my legs and a less-than-favourable reference, not worth the paper it was written on. For I had screwed up big time and had paved the way for a long an arduous journey through life - picking up dead-end-jobs and going nowhere.

Oh how bad choices we make in the early part of our lives can so easily map out our destinies. If only we could have the foresight to see the consequences of our actions and feel the pain we will one day cause ourselves and inflict on others. I would give anything to be able to live a life with a clean slate - to be able to choose the job I want and to be able to work towards a career without the worry of my past spoiling it. But what is done is done. The oppressive atmosphere on Teesside created by high unemployment was increasing. On top of this, recent years had affected my mother and me badly so we decided to leave the area. In 1983, we moved to her hometown of York. We managed to get a house exchange through what was then *Langbaurgh Borough Council*.

Another family had wanted to move to grangetown from York, so it was a straight swap. We moved to Harrington Avenue in Tang Hall, to start a new life - or so we thought. There was so many repairs needed doing to our new shabby council house and after some persuading, we managed to get *York Council* to do something about it.

It was evident that *York Council* was a different 'kettle of fish' to the council on Teesside. We'd never had this sort of resistance from the council before when it came to asking for basic repairs to be done.

Eventually, they did their job that they were supposed to do, but it was clear that it had been a mistake moving to York. The house was pre-war and had a water beck just outside the back of the garden which used to rise up in the winter bringing rats and mice into the garden.

We were always having to get rid of spiders and other creepy crawlies around the house too which started to get us down. It was a typical example of us thinking 'the grass would be greener' on the other side - only for it to turn out to be not greener - but a nightmare instead.

As the days and weeks passed, I became more unhappy about being there. I started going out drinking a lot but I enjoyed the night life. Despite feeling low, I tried to lead a normal life and even managed to find a job at *Russell's Restaurant* as a cleaner. I was always restless and hyper though - always looking for excitement and never satisfied with just having a normal, daily routine. My drinking was causing me to get deeper and deeper into depression. North-Easterners were treated by many of the locals with suspicion and understandably so as there had been a lot of trouble during race meetings as well as at weekends with gangs coming through to get 'wasted' on booze. One day a huge fight broke out in Bootham in the middle of the street between rival gangs where a bicycle was hurled through a shop window and passers-by were left terrified.

Whenever I tell these stories to people, they are shocked to hear such mindless violence could ever occur in such a beautiful City. But it's outsiders that cause it and York has had its fair share of trouble as a result of gangs from other parts of the country - hell bent on wreaking havoc. Sadly, it's a minority as always who do this and then leave it behind. There was a nightclub called, *The Old World* in the early 80s whereby on entry you were asked where you were from and if you had a North-East accent, you were refused entry. If you could prove you lived and worked in York, you were allowed in. I used take my pay slips everywhere with me as other pubs and clubs also had this policy. One day my mother and I walked into a local shop where she asked the owner a simple question who in return gave her a snotty reply. This experience amongst other things had started to build up inside me now.

We had been messed about by the council and spoken to by certain individuals from the so-called upper echelons of society who seem to have taken over York, as though we were beneath them and I'd had enough.

So now with a huge chip on my shoulder, one night after spending part of the night drinking in the *Spotted Cow* pub in Walmgate, ruminating over all the things that had happened since moving to York and how everything had gone wrong in our lives, I decided to take revenge. I went back to that same shop to rob it. So wearing a black balaclava and clenching a large knife I'd bought in a shop in Middlesbrough, I threatened the shopkeeper to hand over money from the till. The next day, it was all over the *York press* which is ironic now because since then I have written for that newspaper many times.

Several days later, while I was visiting friends in Middlesbrough, I confessed all to them. They persuaded me to hand myself in to the police. The police later told me told that I'd never have been caught had I not confessed, but this didn't bother me. I knew what I'd done was wrong and I was prepared to take my punishment. I waited at my friend's house that night for detectives to arrive who seemed to take forever.

Eventually, two officers turned up, arrested me and took me back to South Bank police station. I was led to the reception area and told to stand at the front desk then give my name and details to the desk sergeant. I was searched and asked to empty my pockets where all my belongings such as my wallet, money, comb and so on, were all placed on the desk, and then listed which I then signed for.

My belt was removed and I was then taken into another room where my fingerprints were taken. I could never relax for this. An officer takes hold of one of your forefingers then presses and rolls it across a black ink pad. And then while still holding on, rolls it on to a sheet of white paper which illustrates which finger print goes where. Then you press both thumbs into the ink and then on to the paper. You're supposed to relax your fingers, but I always tensed them. It used to take several attempts to get it right. The police must have thought I was doing it on purpose. I was taken along a smelly dingy corridor which housed several cells. Someone was hammering on his cell door shouting, 'Boss, Boss'! 'Can I make a phone call'? I was told to take off my shoes which were then left outside the cell door. Police custody is one of the worst stages of the arrest process because it's like being in solitary confinement - something I would one day become acquainted with. I was locked in a smelly old cell which had a lingering stench of sweat, food and decay.

The walls and doors were daubed with years of graffiti; the bed was a solid wooden bench on top of which were two carefully folded grey woollen blankets. I used one of the blankets as a pillow as there wasn't a proper one. The cell windows were a thick, frosted glass that offered no view of anything outside my four walls and because it was permanently dark inside, there was no way of knowing what time of day it was.

Every half hour or so, I would hear the spy-hole cover being moved as they kept checking on me. All there was to do all day was sleep which was only interrupted occasionally when my solicitor turned up to go through my statement with me.

Whatever time of day you were arrested, even if it was in the early hours of the morning, a duty solicitor would be called out to see you, if you requested one. After going through my statement, my solicitor tried to get me bail which was at the discretion of the duty police sergeant.

Their decision was based on if they thought you would do a runner, or if emotions in the community were running so high you should be kept in for your own safety. I was kept in as I was being transferred to York the next day. Whenever you're waiting to be transferred somewhere, it's a long and mind-numbing wait.

But once you're on the move and sat in that vehicle, a huge relief comes over you that you're out of those dreadful cells - even if you are handcuffed throughout the entire journey. I was collected by two police officers from York the next day. I can't remember what time of day it was when they arrived, but it seemed like an eternity waiting for them. One of them was a Teessider, so he'd taken the opportunity to visit his hometown. On the long journey back to York, I was handcuffed to him in the back of an unmarked police car and we had a bit of 'banter' on the way. I was surprised at their easy going manner and I remember thinking that they were actually okay.

As we travelled along Normanby trunk road, who would have believed it? But we were actually pulled over by the police. It was comical because they were accusing the officers I was with, of running a red light, and were clearly trying it on. The copper I was cuffed to just raised our hands showing him the handcuffs. 'We're escorting a prisoner', he said. The red faced young copper apologised and sheepishly went back to his car with his tail between his legs. I creased up laughing when the copper handcuffed to me muttered some insulting remark aimed towards the young copper, which I cannot repeat.

Back at York police station, I was questioned by detectives, then the next day taken back to our house in Tang Hall handcuffed to one of them, while he and one of his colleagues searched my bedroom to recover the weapon and balaclava. They confiscated those and also an SLR army issue rifle magazine which I held on to as a souvenir from my army days.

This was classed as a weapon and added to my record. I was just relieved that my mother was out that day, as it would have upset her seeing me handcuffed to a huge copper. My mother couldn't understand why I had gone from being such a quiet stable, nice lad to a criminal overnight. She also took offence at the detective telling her one day I was evil. He'd based his judgement from the two days he'd known me.

The next day I appeared before York Magistrate's court where my solicitor was certain I'd get bail this time with it being my first offence. A group of us were appearing in court that day, so we were all handcuffed to one another and then taken to a white mini-bus where we sat in the back in two rows. When we were handcuffed to each other, the person to the right would have his right arm cuffed to the other person's right arm so his right arm went across in front of him.

The idea of this was to make it difficult for us to make a run for it. As we drove through the streets of York, a real old-school bobby who was one of our escorts, suddenly said to me, 'Were you in the army then Honeywell'? 'Yes', I replied. 'What regiment were you in'? he said. 'RAOC', I answered. 'Oh, so you weren't in the army then!' he quickly responded. The others gave a snigger - as though they could've had even the slightest inclination what we were talking about. I just laughed. I didn't take offence at the old bobby's quip because I knew he was trying to keep everyone's spirits uplifted. I guessed he'd have had some stories to tell if you could've ever got him to talk about them.

One of the things that did stand out to me was how they all had banter with one another. The police obviously dealt with these same individuals on a regular basis and both parties had struck up this bizarre familiarity. The others thought it was highly amusing that I had handed myself in to the police. They were even more entertained when one of the others asked the old-school bobby, 'Would he have been caught if he hadn't handed himself in?' to which the reply was, 'No'.

They all sniggered like school children. I was obviously in the presence of some real morons as the very thought of possessing any conscience was beyond their tiny minds. I was sat next to an Asian police officer, which was a rare sight in those days and not so common these days either. I could see by his expression that he was thinking along the same lines as me. They even mocked him with their attempted witty banter. He told one of the prisoners who'd just lit up a cigarette to stub it out who then defiantly asked the other officer, 'Can we smoke Boss'? He said it was okay so they all laughed at the Asian officer. It was clear to me that he was new to his job and as naive as I was.

He would be learning the hard way as I was about to - but both along very different paths.

As the van drew closer to the courts, a great feeling of sadness come over me as I suddenly caught sight of my mother through one of the windows - hastily trying to cross the road as she headed towards the courts. Once inside the basement of the courtroom building, the handcuffs were removed and we were locked in cells which are always situated below the courtrooms - hence the phrase 'being sent down'. Court sessions were extremely lengthy and boring. They usually started around 10.00am and finished around 4.30pm. Whether you're due in court at 10.00am, 2.00pm, or 4.00pm, you're stuck in those cells all day which drags on even longer with having to listen to the grinding banter amongst the short-termers such as the burglars and thieves continually jabbering about what short sentences they were expecting.

They would painfully repeat how they'll be home in time for Christmas and how they can do their 'bird' (sentence) 'standing on their heads'. Their voices would grind on me like that gnawing sensation of a dentist's drill. Each one excitedly chattered away without pausing for a single breath - feeling absolutely no remorse about their crimes or victims, or any thought for those sat in the same cell facing years of incarceration. The hours dragged on so much, you find yourself actually reading all the graffiti scribbled around the cell walls and ceilings over and over by those who have gone before you over bygone months and years.

You keep listening out for the clanking of the guard's keys in the hope that it's now your turn in the dock or meal time - anything that will break the painful monotony and get you away from the others excruciatingly painful rhetoric. I couldn't understand how they were able to talk so easily about everything with a sort of skip in their step - getting a buzz from the whole experience.

Wasn't being arrested and placed on trial supposed to be painful experience? It worked on me, but for the others, it was merely a game. I was feeling desperately sad and my stomach was so knotted up with anxiety, I didn't want to speak to anyone about anything. The worry must have been etched on my face. But all I really wanted right now was some peace and quiet.

The day dragged on and on until, eventually, it was my turn to make an appearance in the dock. The charges were read out and the prosecuting solicitor, who obviously hadn't done his homework, told the court I had previous convictions. But even though my solicitor completely discredited this and tried his best to put my case to the court by emphasising I was a first time offender; it wasn't enough to get me bail.

The magistrate remanded me in custody for three weeks until my next court appearance. As I was led down the stony steps back to the cells below, I looked directly at my mother who was sat above the stairs and could see the hurt on her face. She looked so unhappy. I was devastated. Many, who choose a life of crime, never take into account how much it hurts others. It's not just the victims of the crimes who suffer; it's also their family and your own family who suffer.

I was powerless to help my mother, I was so depressed. After the court sessions had finished, I was then taken in the van to Thorpe Arch Remand Centre (now Wealstun category 'C' closed prison) near Wetherby, which then was for under twenty-one-year-olds awaiting trial. *En route* I remember we had to stop off at Leeds prison in Armley to drop a prisoner off. As we sat staring out of the van windows, we saw a large prison van, known as a 'sweat box' in the distance.

Sweat boxes are those white vans you see with small, square blacked-out windows on the side. Each window belonged to a metal cubicle which used to get really warm inside and are so small, you can barely move your arms, except to take a drag from a cigarette. Several tough looking prisoners all handcuffed to one another stepped off and as we looked on, one of the police officers with us said, 'There's your real criminals, lads - murderers, and rapists - the lot.'

I remember how bleak it was in the forecourt of the prison and how I dreaded any thought of ever going into a place like that. Because my address was in York, Thorpe Arch was the nearest remand centre to me. Remand time is a period of unrest amongst prisoners, because of the uncertainty of whether you will be found guilty, how long your sentence will be, and when it will actually happen.

At least once you're sentenced, you have a release date which means you can plan ahead. The type of prison that prisoners are sent to and the category they become, depends on their crime and their sentence - the risk of harm they are to the public, and how likely they are to try to escape. The first thing that stood out to me in Thorpe Arch was how much of a doddle it was compared the army glasshouse I'd spent time in two years before. However, it did have other disturbing elements. When I first went in, I was always on edge because I had been expecting to get the same treatment as I'd experienced in the army jail.

I'd jump to attention whenever my cell door opened, but was surprised that nobody shouted orders at you to stand to attention and to run at the double everywhere. You were allowed to walk instead and some of the prisoners even had some friendly banter with the screws (prison officers). The thing I didn't like was that there was so much more going on around me than in the glasshouse, with hundreds of people everywhere.

In the glasshouse there was only me and one other prisoner - three at the most at one point. In reception, we changed into our prison clothes which were blue denims for convicted prisoners and brown for those on remand, awaiting trial. I was taken by a medical screw to the hospital wing for assessment as I had a history of depression.

My cell was at the far end on the right-hand side. There were some very disturbed individuals on that wing. The level of medical knowledge by this medical screw was laughable. He recorded my history of depression as hypotension, which is actually abnormally low blood pressure. If this was a true reflection of the level of medical expertise in prison, I thought, there was no hope for anyone in need of medical assistance.

It was here I first heard the term 'beast' and 'nonce'. These are sex offenders and the word 'nonce' comes from the Latin word *nonsensical,* meaning no sense, because sex crimes make no sense. My naivety was my saviour at times because while I was on the hospital wing, I was unaware that there were 'nonces' sharing my space, unaware that I was mixing with them. Even when I was transferred to the main wing, I hadn't realised what had just happened until it was explained to me.

I knew something wasn't quite right though when I was on the hospital wing. On certain nights we were escorted by one of the hospital staff to the dining hall where we would all watch a film from one of those old fashioned projectors with a film reel. Our little group from the hospital wing would always be taken in last where we were then sat at the back of everyone else. As we all walked in, everyone would turn around and stare at us. This meant absolutely nothing to me at the time until it was later explained to me that it was because some of those with me were in for sex crimes. Because it was a hospital wing, there was a mixture of medical cases including genuine ones such as epilepsy, depression and those with physical injuries. But alongside them were rapists and child-molesters. I was horrified when I learned of this, but with the prison grapevine being as it is, they all knew I was in for violence, so I was safe from accusations.

The main population was more relaxed and I was able to make friends with ordinary lads but there was zero atmosphere. I spent a lot of time in the gym when I got the chance, as it was a great way to keep my mind and body healthy. There were always those who liked to throw their weight around once they developed a bit of muscle. But I had been lifting weights for five years and was quite muscular, so I was lifting heavier weights than most. The male ego really does go wild in prison, but it was our defence mechanism to build on our physiques in the gym - a place where mutual respect and the lion pack mentality is displayed. Prison is a jungle and when it comes to the law of the jungle, you have to parade your strengths and hide your weaknesses.

A lot of the lads used to train like mad men on the weights trying and build as much size as possible thinking it would make people wary of them. It's a protection thing - a 'don't mess with me' mentality. You could see a sort of metamorphoses taking place as they grew in size trying desperately to look tough. I noticed this mostly amongst young prisoners rather than the older ones during both my 1980s and 1990s sentences.

A major difference in the 90s though, was that drugs were finding their way into prisons - including steroids for muscle growth - which brought a whole new set of problems. The nature of prison is that everything is magnified and seems far worse than it really is. Prisoners overreact at the slightest things. All it takes is an innocuous remark, or a rumour that gets completely blown out of proportion and all hell can break loose.

The boredom and frustrations brought on by incarceration, leads to violence, quite often completely unprovoked. You just have to get your head down and do your bird and not allow anyone to intimidate you. One day, out of the blue, my father turned up to visit me and burst into tears in the visiting room. I can't say if they were genuine tears or tears of self-pity. I'll never know.

Then three weeks after going into Thorpe Arch, I was bailed at York Magistrates on condition I resided at South Bank bail hostel, near Middlesbrough. My mother was still living in York, so although they'd sent me back to where I originally lived, she was living over fifty miles away.

CHAPTER EIGHT

ON THE RUN

South Bank Bail Hostel, near Middlesbrough was situated opposite an old church. I can't remember how many were staying there, but there were about twelve people, all ages waiting for their trial dates. I was bored to death here. I was never good at dealing with boredom. I always had a very low boredom threshold. Apart from the dreariness of the place, I didn't much like the way it was run either, or the other residents' petty ways.

Apart from being mind numbing, there were a few in there I couldn't stand to be in the same room as. They all had irritating habits such as their own special place at the dinner table and if anyone sat in their chair they'd 'spit their dummy out'. It was pathetic. There was a television room, pool table and a few weights I used to train with. The gym instructors were okay and this was the only part of it I liked.

We had dormitories with about five beds and there was a curfew at 11.00pm. I used to go and visit my Uncle Billy who lived in nearby Queen Street, or I'd go to the Victoria pub which was practically next door to the hostel. I knew I wouldn't settle at the hostel though.

From day one, I was restless and anxious about everything. I was worried about what would happen to me at court which made it much harder to settle, but eventually, I made the whole situation worse anyway. One of the other lads, who was a skinhead from Darlington called John, was also fed up being in there so we started knocking around together. We used to go to the pub and plan how to get out of there. One day we took a trip to Darlington to do a planned robbery which went wrong and it was then that John stabbed someone with my knife. We made it back to Middlesbrough on the train and back to the hostel before the curfew. We were at the breakfast table the next morning when it came over the radio saying that two men were being hunted by police.

There was a few knowing glances around the table from the others, but it was terrible what we'd done. One of the 'grasses' in the hostel told the staff who then called the police. The next day, two detectives from Darlington came to see us and we were questioned at South Bank Police station. I just wanted this to go away, but I knew we were in the thick of it now and there was no turning back.

After what seemed like endless questioning, back at the hostel, John and I both decided it was time to go on the run. We had this mad idea about hitch-hiking to London which we thought was paved with gold. On the day we decided to break out, we cut the alarm wires which were upstairs in one of the dormitories, so when it was time to make our escape, we'd make our getaway smoothly and quietly.

When nightfall arrived, we sneaked out of the top window and made our way down the steps. We headed for Middlesbrough when John got this dumb idea to burgle someone's house. I always hated burglaries because it's someone's home that's being invaded. I refused to have anything to do with it, so I waited outside while he insisted on doing a 'creep' (night-time burglary).

Shortly after he broke in to a house, I heard a raucous yell from inside the house and as I looked across, all I saw was John leaping down the stairs two or three at a time followed by the man he'd try to burgle. We ran like hell to get away and hid in some nearby bushes for hours. Shortly afterwards a police car started scouring the area which passed us several times. But when we decided to make our move, we were stopped within seconds and questioned. It was obvious to the police officer that we matched the description of who they were looking for so he radioed through to his colleagues. The next thing we knew, a police van came screeching around the corner to take us away to Middlesbrough Police station. As we were arrested and led to the rear of the van, one of the more Neanderthal type officers said, 'Get in c--t.'

Just after being taken in to custody, John decided to be awkward by not telling the police his name - being defiant to the end. We were asked to remove our belongings and then locked up. The two Darlington detectives who had questioned us at South Bank turned up the next day and took us back to Darlington Police cells which were the worst cells I'd ever been in and where I spent the longest time in police custody.

At first, John and I were in the same cell, and then we were separated. John was pressurising me to take the blame for the stabbing. But I was only going to admit my part of it. Thankfully, John finally confessed that it was he who used the knife which made things a lot easier for me. He thought that he could intimidate me into taking the blame so he could avoid getting a lengthy sentence which he would, because of his previous convictions.

He thought that because I was a first offender, I should admit to something I hadn't done and accept a few more years inside, because with him being a repeat offender, he would get a long stretch. I even had his cousin, who was also serving time, trying to get me to do it.

He was nagging me on the way to court in the prison 'sweat van' one day. I stuck my neck out, but where I had started out with being charged with one attempted robbery before I met John, I was now being charged with two attempted robberies, a wounding charge and a burglary. But I didn't think I should be charged with crimes I hadn't committed. Nevertheless, I was still an accomplice which was enough for me to be charged for my part in being there. I had to take it on the chin.

After entering our pleas at Darlington Magistrates, I was taken to Low Newton Remand Centre in County Durham and because John was older than me, he was taken to Durham prison.

CHAPTER NINE

THE 'NEWBIE'

When someone first came in to prison, they'd usually been living a reckless life consisting of drink and drugs, so they slept for hours a day at first to regain energy - exhausted by their lifestyle. Some are very quiet and wary, especially if it was their first time in prison. Then as they recovered some energy from days of sleeping and settling into their new surroundings, they'd start to find their own sets of friends.

The days went by fast really as long as I didn't keep thinking about my release date. Low Newton was a remand prison situated in Durham County, very much like Thorpe Arch, but I preferred Low Newton to Thorpe Arch. My trouble was, I was so naive, but I had to change quickly - otherwise I would never survive. Low Newton had exactly the same routine as Thorpe Arch, but it was more local so I could get more visits.

My mother had now moved back to Middlesbrough after exchanging houses again with the same family as before, so she was living back in the same house. My aunt and uncle would bring my mother through for regular visits. Prisoners were always brought into the visiting room first after being searched, then once everyone was sat at tables, the visitors were brought in.

The room was quite large and there was a small canteen where visitors could go and buy cups of tea, sweets and biscuits. This was when you could enjoy a bit of normality with a few simple luxuries you had always in the past taken for granted. You got to drink from a real cup instead of the usual plastic pint mug, eat a donut and some goodies. I felt sorry for my mother, especially one day when she cried seeing me sat opposite to her at the table. You can have more privileges while you're on remand because prisoners haven't been convicted at that point and are technically innocent although it's hardly evident with the long hours of bang-up and treatment from some of the screws and other staff.

Once you're sentenced, your privileges are reduced. So while on remand, we made the most of it, getting extra tobacco, sweets and so on brought in by your visitors or sent in by parcel. It was quite exciting when your cell door was opened and a screw told you to go and sign for a parcel someone had sent you. While I was living in York, I befriended a gay couple who ran a local store close to us in Tang Hall. I was touched when they sent me a parcel containing a huge bar of chocolate for Christmas.

We were all in single cells which measured nine feet by five feet as did all the other cells I was ever in. It had a single bed, a cork board on the wall and there was a blue table and chair where I ate my meals. Heat radiated from large heavy steel pipes situated underneath the barred windows that passed through everyone's cells. They were useful for drying our underwear and socks on, and also for passing things through to one another through the three inch wide gap.

Being a new lad or 'newbie' as they say today, someone shouted through the pipes, 'Do you want a 'tab'? (cigarette). The most commonly used cigarettes in prison were roll-ups made from cigarette papers and tobacco. I'd spent all day with this joker and his mates in the holding cells during transit from court. So thinking it was a nice gesture, I said, 'Yeah'! Thanks'! It was passed through the gap from two cells down. And as I carefully lit the cigarette, it ignited like a fire cracker singing my mouth. I then heard hysterical laughter coming from him and his mate next door. The idiot had crushed match sulphur and put it inside the cigarette paper so when I lit it, it would burn my mouth. It was this sort of immaturity and stupidity from certain individuals that made my time drag out even more. I could cope with being locked up. It was some of the idiots around me I couldn't cope with.

Not long after, I was moved to share a cell with someone and I started talking to him about escaping. Whenever I used to go on exercise I'd check out the fences and the area to see how difficult it would be to break out. Then of course there were the Alsatian dogs to consider who would tear me apart if they got me. It was rumoured that the fences could be smashed through if you used something heavy enough.

I decided to take my chances and do it the old fashioned way. I managed to make a sharp instrument from a tin I'd taken from the cleaners' cupboard and started chipping away around the bricks which was surprisingly easy. Then I would cover it with paste each night before resuming the digging the next night. I didn't get far because my cellmate who was taken to court one day decided to 'grass' (inform) on me. He must have known he was going to get bail. The next thing I knew, two screws wandered into the cell and went straight to the area where I'd been digging.

Before I knew it, I was sat in solitary confinement where you have absolutely no possessions whatsoever in the cell. When you go in front of the governor to discover your fate, two screws stand either side facing you, close enough to feel their breath. The idea is to protect the governor from you in case you decide to lunge at him or her. A slight balding man with rimmed glasses asked me why I tried to escape to which I replied, 'I was scared of being raped Sir'. Something had stuck in my mind from months before I was sent to prison. I had seen a very disturbing scene from the classic film *Scum* where a young lad was gang raped.

Also my co-accused, John, had taunted me that when I got to Durham prison, I could be raped. But I realised he was just trying to scare me because I'd refused to take the 'rap' (blame) for the stabbing he'd done. He even told me that Durham prison was overrun with rats. I asked the screw who was handcuffed to me on the journey from court to Durham after we were sentenced if it was true, to which he replied, 'Only the two legged kind'.

John's attempt to scare me though, worked. The fear of being raped was enough for me to try and break out of Low Newton. The governor just looked up at me and said, 'I don't think you'll find that will happen'. He then gave me two weeks loss of privileges, three days in solitary confinement and two weeks in the block over Christmas. Solitary is a single bare cell and the block is a segregated wing consisting of other prisoners.

In solitary, you were only allowed your mattress after 8.30pm, and then every morning you had to take it out and lean it against the wall outside your cell until night time. This was just an added punishment so you couldn't lie around on your bed all day. This rule was abolished during my next stint in solitary in 1997 when Europe outlawed it.

In the block, however, you are allowed some of your belongings such as books, writing materials and it's not as harsh as solitary. But the boredom is still horrendous. The block kept you away from the main population and deprived you of privileges such as association (socialising period). In another part of the prison was a grim looking stone building known as the 'psycho cell' which one of the cleaners showed me one day. It was used for the most disturbed and violent offenders. It had steps leading up to the top of it. So I climbed them and looked down through a thick glass roof into what I can only describe as the grimmest dungeon I've ever seen. Down inside, was a stone slab for a mattress - I assumed. And the walls were just cold, thick solid stone.

My visits were also stopped while I was in the block until the governor took pity on me one day and allowed me a visit from my mother with it being so close to Christmas. She turned up with some Christmas presents for me but had them handed back to her. 'Sorry, he's been a naughty boy', one of the screws politely said to her. I could see the embarrassment and sadness on her face as he handed them back to her. I felt gutted that I had caused her all this grief. But she held on to them for me until the day I was released. I would go back to my cell after a visit feeling wrecked inside.

Emotions always ran high at Christmas-time in prison. There was a fight in the dinner queue one day and as one of the screws intervened, he said, 'Come on now, it's Christmas.' We thought this was ironically amusing. Visits were more strained than the rest of year and everyone felt they were missing out on all the festivities and obviously if they had children, they suffered even more.

You thought more about family and friends and all the celebrations you were missing out on. Though I have to say, once in prison, you find out who your real friends are. A lot of so-called friends forget about you, or make lots of excuses and empty promises. Some just decide not to have anything to do with you anymore. Even in prison, there was a term known as, 'prison talk' which was a load of empty promises from other prisoners who would say they'd keep in touch and meet up with you once you were out. But once they began to taste freedom, you never heard from them again. Only the lifers I became good friends with stayed in contact throughout as well as one or two others.

On January 19 1984, I was in the dock at Teesside Crown Court for sentencing with my co-accused John standing before Judge Angus Stroyne. There was no jury trial because we were pleading guilty. It seemed an eternity, listening to all the legal jargon from men and women wearing black gowns and horse-hair wigs. Some prisoners were very knowledgeable with legal know-how and got right into all the ins and outs of it all - the court procedures and how the system worked.

I was sentenced to thirty months youth custody and John got six years imprisonment. I glanced at John as his sentence was handed out and the emotion that came over his face said it all. He went white because he hadn't been expecting to get that long. And he'd wanted me to take the 'rap' for him?

We were both then sent to Durham Prison. John was later transferred to Frankland - category A - prison. I later heard he'd slashed another prisoner with a broken jam jar.

CHAPTER TEN

KEY TO THE DOOR

Whereas eighteen is, these days considered the age of maturity, it used to be twenty-one when you became an adult in Britain. As an adult, you were considered free to come and go as you pleased rather than according to your parents' wishes. Thus, you were now entitled to 'the key of the door'. In my case, I went into prison a twenty-year-old boy and left a twenty-one-year old man, and shortly afterwards, was given the key to freedom by way of parole licence.

Durham Prison is one of the most famous old penal institutions in the United Kingdom. It has been the home of some of Britain's most infamous criminals over the years, including Rose West, Myra Hindley, the Kray twins, Frankie Fraser, and John McVicar. It was also the resting place of a number of men and women executed and buried in its grounds.

I was fascinated by the prison's past and by some of its former infamous inmates such as McVicar - as most of the other prisoners were. I wanted to read McVicar's biography, *McVicar by Himself* (1979), but it was banned by the prison authorities and if anyone was caught with the book, it was confiscated. It was said that this was because, apart from his infamous escape from Durham's E' wing in 1968 which embarrassed the authorities, he 'slags' off the prison and the screws - many of who were still working there when I was in. My first ever job in Durham was working as a cleaner in the 'search tank' where prisoners were frisked before going over to reception. This job was a real easy number just doing a bit of sweeping and polishing for a few hours a day. The screw in charge of me remembered McVicar and this particular screw had a reputation of being a nasty piece of work, but he was alright with me. He told me McVicar was a real handful, but very intelligent. Someone did manage to smuggle McVicar's book in to me eventually by tearing off the front page.

But when one of the screws 'sussed it', the book was removed and put in my property for when I was released - which had mysteriously vanished - I noticed - when that day arrived. But I had read it by then and was inspired by McVicar's educational achievements during his time in prison. It really made me want to do the same so when I was released in 1985 I tried to follow his example.

I was dreading my thirty months ahead, while others just took it as an occupational hazard - eager to get on the wing and see all their buddies. After being processed, signing for our property, getting a bath, and exchanging our clothes for our new prison attire, we were taken to our cells. My new clothes consisted of two blue tee-shirts, a green denim jacket, two blue-and-white-striped shirts, an ill fitting pair of half-mast blue denims, three pairs of socks, underwear and a pair of hard black shoes that had been worn by hundreds before me. And would give you blisters if not cripple your feet. YPs all wore green denim jackets whereas the over-twenty-one-year-old prisoners, known as, 'cons', wore blue denim jackets.

We weren't allowed to mingle with the 'cons' so our different coloured jackets were to distinguish us from them. YPs all lived on the same landing, went to work, the gym and shower together. We were given a plastic mug, knife, fork and spoon, a tooth brush, tooth powder, some *White Windsor* soap, two towels, two blankets, two pillow cases and two sheets. By the time we were processed and taken to our cells, it was usually quite late because we had spent all day at court. So by the time we'd gone through the prison reception ordeal, the day was over. Once we were on 'D' wing, we were allowed a free reception letter and some money to buy a few items or toiletries. We were also entitled to a reception visit, which was an extra visit you could request where your friends or family could come and see you as soon as they could get there. In the 'tuck shop' which was the old gallows, I bought a half-ounce of *Golden Virginia* tobacco, a box of matches, some *Rizla* cigarette papers and a penny chew. We were then led up the steep metal stairs to the second landing, 'the twos,' where the first man was let into his cell.

Eventually, we were on the third landing, 'the threes,' where my cell was situated. Reality hit me as my door was unlocked and I looked into this tiny cold dark room. I entered what was now to become my new home. The door slammed shut behind with me with a deafening sound that echoed across the whole landing.

There was a single, blue hospital bed with a striped mattress and a single pillow. I threw all of my bedding on to it and absorbed my new surroundings. In the corner, there was a triangle-shaped table with a blue top and another small table next to it to have my meals at. The cell window was so high that I couldn't reach it without standing on the table. But when I sat on the wooden chair and gazed up towards it, I could see the stars which made me wish I could stand outside in the cold night air.

There was a single light bulb, which I couldn't turn on because the switch was on the other side of the door. When it turned 10:00 pm (lights out), you were plunged into total darkness. I was alone in the dark with only my thoughts, then like replaying a video, my mind drifted back recalling the day's events, which now seem to be a far distant memory. It was difficult to get to sleep and every so often, I could hear the spy-hole cover move slightly as a screw took a peek to make sure all was well. Thinking of my family, I felt a deep sadness grow inside me that they were so far away and I will not be able to get close to them for quite a while. I started to realise that I would not have my mother's home-cooking to look forward to for a long time and I wouldn't be able to watch late films with her like we used to.

I thought about how she was now alone in her house back in Middlesbrough. She told me years later, how just after I was sentenced, she went across to a cafe and bought a coffee which lasted an hour - as she sat there numbed with shock - staring into space. For her son who had always been such a good kid in the past, was in now one of the most notorious prisons in the country.

I must have drifted off to sleep, because, suddenly, I was woken by a bright light glaring in my face as the screws stomped along the landings switching everyone's lights on and peeping through our spy-holes. It was morning and time to get up. It was a cold winter's day and as I forced myself out of bed and on to the icy cold floor, I could hear the loud piercing echoes of screws shouting to one another, 'All ready on the twos, Mr. Pendlworth?' 'All ready on the twos, sir!' came the response, 'All ready on threes, Mr Stevens?' All ready on threes, Sir!' Then the order followed, 'Okay, unlock!'

The doors were unlocked and left slightly ajar. I popped my head out, where I could see lines of men wearing blue tee-shirts and blue denims, sleepily dragging themselves along the landing at 6:30 am. I could see they were all carrying plastic chamber pots to slop out their human waste that had accumulated through the night. And in the other hand, bowls to collect water to wash their grubby hands and faces in and white plastic jugs to collect drinking water.

In those days we didn't have toilets and washbasins in the cells, so we had to do all our toilet needs into these plastic chamber pots. Three times a day we were unlocked to dispose of its contents in the daily ritual known as 'slop out' where we emptied our pots into large sinks situated in the recess area. Tempers were frayed as it was far too early in the morning to be suddenly woken by a bright light and a bang on the door followed by a screw bellowing, 'Slop out!'

There was one toilet in the recess area at the foot of each landing and if you could get there before someone else beat you to it, you made the most of it. I never thought using a toilet could ever be such a luxury, but it was at times like that, we realised how much we'd taken everything in life for granted.

The disadvantage of the toilet though, was that the door was only waist height, so while everyone was crammed in the packed recess area slopping out, they could see you sat on the throne (toilet). There was sort of a mutual respect amongst one another though. We always gave one another as much privacy as possible. And whenever you had to use the chamber pots in your cells, your cellmate would read a newspaper, or if he was on his bed, he would turn and face the wall to give you some privacy. The reason we didn't have toilets in those days was because Durham dated from the Victorian era and wasn't originally designed to have toilets.

Some of the prisoners who couldn't stomach the stench of their waste festering at the foot of their beds, would try and persuade a screw to let them use the toilet in the recess area. But because some power mad screws wouldn't allow it, they used to do their business on a newspaper, fold it up like a parcel and sling it through the bars. Then some other poor mug would end up having to scoop it up the next day. If someone had bad guts and desperately needed to go, they would plead with the screws to let them use the recess toilet, some who were okay and would allow them to use it, and some who just wouldn't. Sometimes, if I was coming back from a visit or work, I would see rows of 'fallen tallies' (metal number plates), where prisoners had pressed their buzzers to get the screws attention who were standing at one end of the landing ignoring them all.

As the morning ritual unfolded, once we'd collected our water and slopped out, a screw would come around with a wooden box which had all our individually named razor blades inside. The paper which our razor blades were wrapped in had our names written on because we used the same blade every morning - until it was replaced with a new one at the end of the week.

You always had to be clean shaven unless you made a formal application and were granted permission to grow facial hair. It was classed as 'changing your appearance'. Shortly afterwards, our razors were collected back, but while we were waiting for the screw to come back for them, we quickly used this period to slice our matches into four quarters so they would last longer. It was quite a skill to be able to slice a match into four while making sure the sulphur remained intact.

As my first eventful day in Durham continued, to my relief, I saw some familiar faces from Low Newton. There was Elvis who I'd shared a cell with who was 'banged up' nearby and a couple of the others who all looked as though reality was just kicking in for them too. As I walked down the flights of metal stairs for breakfast, I recall seeing what looked like a female prisoner strutting along the landing like a model on a catwalk. He had a certain rapport with the screws and other prisoners and all you could hear was, 'Laura!' 'Laura!' echoing from all directions. Laura was the first transsexual I had ever seen and from what I was seeing was one very popular prisoner.

He was going through a whole sex change apparently, using hormone medication and so on. You could see he loved all the attention he received as much as everyone enjoyed having such a great character around to brighten up the long dull days. On the big shower day, Laura had to have a bath, segregated from the rest of us. I was told it was because of his body changes and that he would get excited being around us, but as I have said, prison gossip is even worse than gossip 'on the out'.

He was always in and out of prison for soliciting in Newcastle's West End on a regular basis, but he hadn't been released long, when one day, while gazing through my cell window, I saw a screw escorting him back in again. Someone yelled from his cell window, 'What you in for Laura?' 'Murder!' he replied.

He was charged for murdering his father after stabbing him with a potato peeler, but was eventually acquitted. He was a regular face in the prison and it would have been difficult to distinguish him from a real woman had we not known who he was. Every Sunday morning the Chapel was packed with prisoners wanting a glimpse of Laura who basked in all the attention he was getting. Well, I very much doubt they were all in Chapel because they'd all suddenly seen the light. It was also an extra hour out of our cells.

The night before being released, I waved across to Laura's cell to say goodbye and he waved back. Years later, I heard that Laura had died from AIDS in Newcastle. Those who didn't have a job were locked up for twenty-three hours a day. And the only break from the endless monotony of 'bang-up' was 'exercise'. Around 11.00am each morning, a screw would shout, 'exercise'! 'Press your buzzers if you want to go on exercise!!'

'Exercise' was a daily ritual where we were all given an hour to stretch our legs and meet one another. We would walk around in circles, around the perimeter of the 'exercise yard'. We were never allowed to mingle in more than three, walk anti-clockwise or stop walking.

One day, while we were all congregated at the entrance leading to the yard, a child abuser from the VP (vulnerable prisoner) wing (situated near the entrance), rang his bell and asked one of the screws if he could come on exercise with the rest of us.

The screw strongly advised against this as it could only cause trouble. But he was insistent - wanting to exercise his right to choose. A very reluctant prison officer unlocked his cell door and allowed him to come out on the yard with the rest of us.

As he joined the crowd at the entrance, I could see him being pushed and shoved while one or two gave him a dig. Once on the yard, everyone started taunting him so he started throwing stones and shouting obscenities at us. Eventually the screws could see a potential riot brewing and before long took him back to his cell.

Prison doesn't have a particular type of person as one might expect. Prisoners come in all shapes and sizes, nationalities, ages and backgrounds. There were murderers, shop lifters, rapists, television licence dodgers and some who preferred spending six weeks a year in prison rather than paying child maintenance. It was a real mixed bag of people.

The place was full of characters, some of who scared me and fascinated me at the same time. There was one ruthless well-known villain called Freddie Mills (Fred the head) who was very loud and as large as life. He was able to walk around as he pleased and the screws never challenged him. He would go berserk at night hammering on his cell door, releasing his pent up anger, but was never 'nicked' for it.

Four armed robbers came in once having just received twelve-years each for a well executed heist on a security van. They had stolen £95,000 which hadn't been recovered. Buried beneath the ground somewhere, they decided to send a relative to rescue it. Unfortunately for them, the police were waiting and recovered the lot. The 'digger' got eighteen months, while the others now had a long stretch ahead of them for nothing.

As I got to the breakfast queue, a huge bloke who was as 'camp' as they come, was eyeing up the new young prisoners. He was in charge of the cleaners who also served food to prisoners alongside some of the screws.

There was old Albert who had spent his lifetime in and out of the place since his first sentence of seven years for stealing a shirt from a store. He was about seventy-two-years old and would always run up to you and 'natter away' as you walked along. You'd see him every day walking along 'D' wing picking up 'dog-ends' off the floor which he'd collect until he had enough to make a new cigarette.

Albert was respected by the screws due to his age, the fact he was harmless and because they'd known him for so long. We all loved characters. He eventually died in the prison, which may sound sad, but he was amongst people he regarded as family. To some, prison was home. There was also a well-known tramp who would deliberately get himself sent back to prison by smashing a window or something, as soon as he was released. Towards Christmas, a lot of homeless people would do the same. He saw the prison as his home, which was better than his living conditions on the streets. This is one of the most tragic things about some of these prisoners' lives. Some of them would rather be in prison than in their alternative living arrangements. It wasn't necessarily because they were shirking responsibility as many would think.

In many cases, it was because of mental illness, or an inability to cope with the outside world, and for some, because prison life was a damn sight better than their home lives. This doesn't mean that prison was easy; it was just that their home lives were so tragic, prison was a much better alternative. One elderly prisoner, who also died in prison, named the governor as his next of kin.

As we shuffled along the queue for our breakfast, we picked up a metal silver tray which had different sections. It had a circular one for your mug, another partition for your knife and fork, then two square sections for your main course and pudding (duff).

There were several long tables where a line of inmate cleaners and screws wearing white coats stood behind slopping food from huge pans on to the prisoner's trays. We got two dollops of porridge that was so thick; you could have used it to cement the cracks in your cell walls. We then got a scoop of sugar, that we saved in a jar as a sort of luxury for when we had our tea at supper time, a boiled egg with four slices of bread and a round knob of butter. At the far end of the line were two large urns filled with coffee and tea.

Meal times were always the highlight of our day. Lunch would consist of something like chicken or vegetable pie, mash and gravy with duff such as sponge and custard, and then at tea time around 4:30 pm, it was a lighter meal with perhaps chips and ham and a different piece of fruit each day. At weekends we used to get these large homemade cookies, which were delicious. Each night around 9:00pm, a screw and a kitchen orderly would come around with a tea urn on top of a trolley and a tray of cookies left over from earlier.

During the day, once we'd all taken our food to our cells, we were locked in. After lunch, everyone's door was unlocked for us to put our trays outside the cell for the cleaners to collect on a trolley. Then the whole prison would go silent for about an hour-and-a-half while everyone took 'forty-winks'. Sometimes you could hear a pin drop apart from the distant sound of soft music coming from transistor radios around the prison. At about 2:00 pm, you would hear doors being unlocked for those who had to go back to work and for some who had visitors.

One thing about prison life which has never changed is that prisoners cannot handle change. It can be the slightest thing from meals being served late; mail not being given out at the usual time or prisoners not being unlocked at their usual time. This can create so much disruption. Prisoners live by daily routine. I have seen trouble brew over things such as the menu being changed. All it takes is the slightest thing and you can have a full scale fight or riot on your hands.

Durham Prison swarmed with cockroaches, due to lack of proper sanitation. The building was over 170 years old and had housed prisoners for many decades. We ate our food in our cells amongst the cockroaches and human waste. I was on the top bunk usually, so my head was near the ventilator through where cockroaches crawled in.

I blocked all the holes up, but they still crawled underneath the cell door.

Sometimes you would move a towel or a book and there'd be one hanging there. Sometimes they appeared in food. I remember seeing the familiar long antennae peeping through my mashed potato one day and another time I ate what I thought was a black chip, but then realised it was in fact half a cockroach. Something that stood out was how everything echoed so loudly through the prison.

Slamming gates and cell doors resonated across the whole building and when you were in your cell, you could hear the screw's boots squeak as they stomped along the rattling metal landings. During visiting hours, you'd listen carefully hoping their footsteps would get closer and that you'd be unlocked because a visitor had come to see you.

You would hear them gradually getting closer to your door, then there would be a brief pause outside as your identity card was checked, then the sound of the keys turn in the keyhole. Our identity cards, which were outside the cell in a wooden slot, were different colours, white for Protestants and red for Catholics. They displayed our name, religion, prison number, sentence and dietary requirements, if there was any.

Every evening we were unlocked for association, when we were allowed about two hours from about 6:00pm and we could leave our cell doors open, mingle with one another, play pool, and watch television. We were 'banged up' again about 8:00 pm, then for the rest of the night, we would chat with one another, read books we could get from the prison library, study, write letters and listen to our radios.

Once a week our laundry was changed when we got fresh linen from the cleaners and then we would all congregate at the huge communal shower room, hand over our dirty clothes to a screw on reception in exchange for fresh clothing which was then placed in a basket to collect after we'd finished showering. I had several different cells during my time in Durham, my first being a single on 'A' wing. A3 was the Young Prisoner (YP) wing. My first cell was like an ice-box. I just sat in it all day with a blanket wrapped around me. From my window, I could see the women's 'E wing' situated on 'H block' where McVicar escaped from. The women used to play their music loud enough for us to hear and they'd wave across and shout to us. I can remember one day the dulcet tones of Bob Marley coming from one of their cell windows filling the air.

And for the short amount of time it lasted, the music took us beyond the prison walls, forgetting where we were. Later, I was moved to another cell where I had a cellmate called Jonesy who really loved himself. He made my life a misery so I requested a cell change. One day in the gym Jonesy was taunting me in front of his mates so I walked over and squared up to him. But he backed down and left me alone after that.

After working in the search tank, I ended up sewing mail bags in the workshops at the rate of two pence a bag. Those who didn't work were given an allowance of £1.13 per week. As well as the workshops that made mailbags for the *Royal Mail*, some of the others produced goal nets for football clubs, and camouflage nets for the army. We used sewing machines whereas the other mailbag shop hand sewed them.

I wasn't interested in this work at all. I just sat there and did nothing. The workplace was run by the one and only female screw in the prison that made some of the men look like pussy cats. She sat perched high on a chair at the head of the room overlooking four rows of prisoners all machining away earning their pittance of pay. One day, she had me escorted back to my cell after noticing I hadn't even attempted to sew a single stitch. She had actually done me a great favour. I got my wish to be moved to another cell which was situated close to the old gallows, callously referred to by the screws as the 'topping shed'. And as I mentioned before, was now the 'tuck shop' where we bought our tobacco and other supplies.

Durham was one of the few prisons to retain a permanent gallows housed at the end of 'D' wing, which was built in 1925. It had two condemned cells, one immediately adjacent to the gallows and one separated from the execution chamber by a corridor that led to the exercise yard. The main condemned cell was formed from three standard cells knocked into one and contained a toilet and washbasin. There was a small lobby between the cell and the gallows room.

A mortuary was available in the yard adjoining the ground floor of the execution chamber. Parts of the execution block still remain to this day, although the condemned cell has been removed and the pit covered over (this area is now used for storage). During my time there and before me, there have been many accounts of paranormal activity and people scared senseless - myself included.

The gallows was situated on the first landing, 'the ones', which was the ground-floor landing. You could see the old trap door above us where we queued. Outside was a steel pedal on which the screw used to keep his foot to prevent the trap doors opening should there be a last-minute reprieve for the condemned prisoner. I could see directly into the cell where prisoners used to spend their final night before execution. The cell was still there and we could see inside it, but what used to be the door on the other side, was now bricked up.

In the early 1990's when the prison was being modernised, the graves of some of those executed were disturbed, including that of Mary Ann Cotton. A pair of female shoes belonging to her were found along with her bones. Several bodies (including Cotton's) were removed and all were later cremated.

All of the inmates hanged in the Twentieth Century were buried alongside the prison hospital wall with only a broad arrow and the date of execution carved into the wall to mark the location of their grave. The original instructions regarding the burial of executed inmates stated that the only clothing an inmate should be buried in was a prison issue shirt. The body was to be placed into a pine box and covered with quicklime and that holes were to be bored into the box before burial. Given the prison's sinister history then, it would seem rather silly to tamper with the unknown. But as I've already said, boredom was the biggest problem in prison, so you have to try and alleviate this somehow.

One night, my cellmate, Tim and I foolishly decided to make our own *Ouija* board. Tim had a lot of experience about this sort of thing, though it was a really stupid idea which turned into a terrifying ordeal. It resulted with tables shaking. We heard screams from inside the cell, objects randomly tipped over as well as some very peculiar disembodied sounds.

I never touched a *Ouija* board again. Those were the longest three sleepless nights I have ever had. I have always had an interest in the paranormal, but you should never play with things you don't understand. I was relieved though that we didn't feel the need to tell the screws what we had done. We had a Scottish screw in charge of us called Mr Assenti who had a 'firm-but-fair' attitude. There were always some screws who just wanted to make prisoner's lives a misery, but you tried to avoid them as much as possible. Mr Assenti was typical old school. The former army sergeant major was short in stature and when he walked, his back was ramrod straight proudly displaying his medal ribbons on his tunic. He was in charge of the YPs and though strict, got a lot of respect from us. After two weeks of sewing mailbags, my brain was so numbed, I wanted a different job. So I asked one of the nicer screws, Mr Coates, if he could help.

A few days later, a small slip of paper was slid underneath my cell door telling me I was to attend education classes the next day. This would drive me to knuckle down and study which McVicar's book had inspired me to do. But it would be many years later before I actually made some real educational achievements. Classes consisted of basic learning skills to accredited qualifications. Then during the summer, I was shipped out to Castington Young Offenders Institute in Northumberland situated next to Acklington's Category 'C' adult prison, and I detested it.

A lot of the other YPs acted like children. I think my short but memorable stint in the army must have helped me grow up a bit, because I always seemed to have an older head than a lot of the others. But then again, a lot were several years younger than me and I would soon be too old to be in there anyway.

During my stay, fires were lit every night and cells were smashed up. It was a world away from Durham.

Young offender institutions lack any form of maturity, so violence is even more spontaneous. Young prisoners are still entering adulthood and want to prove themselves, so bullying was rifer amongst the younger prisoners who wanted to gain fearsome reputations. I just wanted to be back amongst the mature convicts.

It was only a month before my twenty-first birthday after which they could no longer hold me in a young offender's prison, so it was a pointless transfer in the first place. I'd have to be moved back to Durham once I was twenty-one anyway. That suited me fine though, because Durham, even with all its downsides, was where I preferred to be. Even though in Castington, we had toilets and washbasins in our cells, a nice dining hall to have our meals in and jobs to go to, I just couldn't stand the place. I wanted to get out of there as soon as possible.

On the positive side of things, they had an excellent gym and we were allowed to run laps around the inside of the fence where there was a path. It was a stifling summer - one of the hottest summers I can remember. The overpowering heat from the sun would sometimes beam through the cell windows, yet we weren't allowed to hang a cover or blanket up to block out the sunlight. We couldn't escape the direct sunlight. I developed a terrible migraine headache. It felt as though someone was sticking a sharp object through my eye socket.

The pain was excruciating, but I couldn't leave the cell or hide from the direct rays of the scorching sun. I then became so ill I started vomiting.

Then one Sunday, unable to suffer the pain anymore, I rang the bell and requested to see the doctor. I was warned that if the doctor had to make a special journey to come out see me, I'd be confined to my cell for three days because it was a Sunday and therefore a great inconvenience for him. But I was in too much pain to care. When he eventually turned up, he prescribed a few aspirin tablets and then had me sent back to my cell.

I was then punished for being unwell and causing such an inconvenience, but it was normal to be treated with contempt by the prison medical and civilian staff. The mentality of these fools was to confine me to my cell for three days where I was in constant pain from the direct sunlight for even longer periods of time.

At least before then, I could go to the dining hall for my meals to escape the heat for a short time whereas now I was having all my meals brought to me in my cell. Prison medical care for inmates was diabolical. Rude, uncaring people ran the prison medical centre. I despised the prison civilian medical staff. I reviled no prison officer or other member of staff as much as these people. If you were on medication, it was slammed down in front of you when you went to collect it. You could see the hate on their faces as they spoke to you like dirt. One the nicer screws, Mr O'Brian was on duty most of the time and we struck up some good banter. He was from my 'neck of the woods' in Eston and years later, I often saw him in the Labour Club at weekends when we'd have a catch up.

Prisoners were given aspirin water for every type of ailment, even some of most serious injuries. I once remember a prisoner being given aspirin water after he broke his arm. Aspirin water which was one or two aspirins crushed into water was the answer to everything. During my time in prison in the 1990's, some of my gums became infected causing painful toothache, but so bad was the health care, my teeth were left to rot until I was released when I had to have several removed.

Once I turned twenty-one, they finally transferred me back to Durham. After Castington, I looked forward to returning to Durham Prison. And shortly after getting back, I got a job in the kitchen which was one of the most popular jobs in any prison. The kitchen in Durham was infested by cockroaches, as were the cells and the rest of the prison. If you moved a bag of flour you would suddenly see swarms of them scuttling across the kitchen floor. But the job brought with it certain privileges, such as extra portions of food, more than one shower a week, and more changes of clothing. We always wore white tee-shirts instead of the usual blue ones and the kitchen screws always wore white coats. Like in most prisons, the screws who worked everyday with prisoners - whatever the work was - tended to develop better relationships with prisoners, compared to those who only worked on the landings. The 'work-screws' used to treat their prisoner side-kicks more like workmates developing a rapport and mutual respect. Prisoners and prison officers in the workplace had a different kind of relationship and interaction than the rest.

Several months earlier, I had applied to be considered for parole. The term 'Jam Roll' is English prison slang for parole where prisoners are released into the community to serve the remainder of their sentence. In criminal justice systems, parole is the supervised release of a prisoner before the completion of their sentence in prison. This differs from amnesty or commutation of sentence in that parolees are still considered to be serving their sentences, and may be returned to prison if they violate the conditions of their parole.

One day while lying on my bed, I could hear several prisoners talking outside waiting to be let into their cells. Whenever you came back from work or a visit, a screw escorted you back to the landing. You would then walk to your cell and wait for the landing screw to come along and open the door to let you in. If there were no screws around, one of us would have to go to the office and ask to be let in. I didn't like to do this because the screws office was a place of hostility. Whenever you needed to go to the office for anything, there was usually a half-a-dozen screws sitting around doing nothing. It felt quite intimidating at times as they would just glare at you while you were trying to talk to the wing officer. The wing officer, a Principle Officer (P.O.) on 'D' wing, was completely unapproachable and always looked as though he was on the verge of a nervous breakdown.

He used to sit at his desk with his bright red face looking as though he was about to explode any moment. His blood pressure must have been sky high. A P.O. was in charge of the wing and the Senior Officer (S.O.), was the next rank down. It was about 4:00 pm, as the lads had just finished work. A sheet of paper suddenly slid underneath my door which I recognised by the logo at the top of the page as being from the Home Office.

I knew it was my parole answer, so bracing myself for bad news, I anxiously read down the page until I saw the words,

'A panel of the parole board considered your case on 19 August 1984 and found you suitable for release on parole licence from 4 September 1984 ....'

Nowadays, you're actually summoned to the office to see the P.O., who presents you with the paper and discusses your conditions with you. But, suddenly, holding this letter in my hand that listed my parole conditions with a recommended date of release, was all I needed and the feeling inside was one of elation.

I had butterflies, my adrenaline was pumping and my mind was racing. I had only been in prison for ten months, but it had seemed like years. It had been my first time in prison for any length of time and the prison environment was so far removed from any kind of reality. For it wasn't just the length of time I'd spent in prison that made me feel so isolated from the outside world; it was also the total absence of anything remotely associated with normality. Prison is a very false environment with a false community and abnormal behaviour where mountains are made out of mole hills and you view things from a totally different perspective than you would outside.

It soon got around the prison grapevine that my parole had come through. My Liverpudlian mate, who I just knew as 'Scouse' and I'd worked with in the mailbag workshop, shouted through my cell door, 'I heard you got your parole mate!' 'Yeah', I shouted back. 'Well done mate,' he said. Each day then became longer than usual, because you're urging your release day on, as it's only days away. This is referred to as being 'gate happy'.

The day before my release, I was taken to reception to check my property and sign for it. I noticed McVicar's book had mysteriously vanished from my property and nobody had a clue what I was talking about when I asked where it was. But at least I could buy my own copy when I was out, I thought. Once I'd signed for my property ready for the following day's release, I knew my parole hadn't been a mistake or a dream; I was actually on my way home. But even though it was official, I couldn't help but think that something could go wrong to spoil it.

I became a bit paranoid, thinking, 'What if someone starts trouble with me? - by someone who is jealous that I'm getting out?' I remember wondering if I should stay in my cell for the next few days in case anything happened to me and my parole got revoked before I was even released. But it never happened and I was unlocked early that morning and told to be ready in ten minutes. They didn't have to hurry me; I'd been ready for hours. I used those ten minutes to say goodbye to 'Scouse' and some of the others. Your release day is an exciting experience; you're on 'cloud nine'. There's no point trying to get any sleep the night before, because you won't manage it. You had your breakfast in the reception area that morning too while paperwork was being prepared. Everyone made sure they ate their breakfast before being released - even if they were too excited to have any appetite - because superstition says that if you don't eat it, you come back to finish it.

One of the others got into an argument with one of the screws behind the desk for some reason and was sent back to his cell. This made me feel very worried that this could happen on your release day. I kept my head down; my mouth shut and just went with the flow.

We were handed long brown cardboard boxes with our names and numbers on containing the clothes we were wearing when we came to prison. We were then told to go and get changed in some cubicles. You were always handed the clothes you were wearing when you were brought in - unless you had served a long time and your body weight had considerably changed - in which case you could claim a clothing grant.

One of the prisoners, a huge black guy, who was well over six-feet tall and of massive build, was arrested at Christmas wearing a Santa Claus costume, so he had to travel home dressed as Santa. There he was sat on a bus in his red and white suit with a big hood and big black boots in the middle of a hot summer's day on what must have been a very long journey.

After we had changed into our clothes, we were handed our property. It was nice to be able to hold my wallet and handle money again. It made me feel like a proper person again because we didn't handle money while in prison. We were given a week's social security money and a green form to take to the job centre where we then signed on for unemployment benefit. My ultimate feeling of excitement was standing anxiously waiting in line at the gate listening for my name to be called out by the screw reading from his list.

As each person's name was called out, the screw would open the door for them to step out. My turn finally came and as I stepped out, I was immediately hit by the fresh air and smell of flowers. The air seems different outside. Within the prison grounds, it's a grey, dull air with a dead ambience. Another lad also from Middlesbrough was released with me so we tagged along together. I got a chance to see the beautiful surroundings of Durham City as we walked towards the train station - soaking in every moment.

Back in Middlesbrough I couldn't wait to get back to see my mother who had stood by me all the way - making those long trips to Durham to visit me every month and writing letters. She had bought me my favourite '45' record out at that time called *Radio Ga Ga* by Queen. Whenever I heard it come over my radio in prison, I would try to get a good signal so I could hear it through the crackling airwaves.

Once I was back in Middlesbrough, I was given instructions to go and `meet my new probation officer, Russell Bruce, who was quite new to his work and around the same age as me. Each week I visited him to talk through what I'd been up to. But my euphoria was short lived as once again I became restless and bored with everything in my life. There were times I would turn up for my appointments under the influence of alcohol.

I was continually drifting, unsure what do with my life. I was drinking too much and being erratic. My parole licence was supposed to last for ten months. Unfortunately, my probation officer was concerned about myself and the safety of others, so he contacted the Home Office. After only six months, the Home Office recalled me back to prison.

CHAPTER ELEVEN

RECALLED

One night around 7:30 pm, while I was getting ready for a night out, there was a sudden knock at the door. When I moved the curtains, I could see from the window a police sergeant. I knew why they'd come. They were unaware of why they had been sent to arrest me, but I knew my parole had been revoked, so I was taken back to Durham Prison to complete another pointless four months. Back at Durham, I went through the same old rigmarole of reception and this time I was taken to 'D' wing where I shared a cell with two others.

Most of the cells had three men sharing the nine-by-five-foot space. I tried to talk to a couple of screws why I was back there to see if it could be appealed against, but it was falling on deaf ears. Shortly after being back, I was transferred to 'C' wing, which was a sort of privileged wing. It had a dartboard, pool table and the usual television room.

Some of the 'cons' played chess and dominoes. It was smaller compared to the main 'D' wing landing which was massive. Prisoners had to be selected for 'C' wing. It was where the red band trustees, most being less violent offenders and short-termers were housed. I don't know why I was taken to 'C' wing, but it was probably because I was only there for four months. Going back to Durham prison had a bad psychological effect on me though. I was so stressed because of the shock of being recalled.

As part of the reception process, the day after I was recalled, I was taken to the see the governor who told me that they would be releasing me again on licence as soon as possible as they felt I didn't need to be in there. This naturally lifted my spirits enormously. My new cell was opposite the main gate and at night, you could hear the pub-goers leaving the local boozer.

I hated my cellmate and he hated me, but it wasn't long to endure. I knocked about with some good guys, such as 'Fingers' who had at some point in his life had some of his fingers chopped off. He was a fellow body builder, so we used to chat about that and the benefits of training. Also within my close circle of friends was another chap called Andy who was the manager of a North East 1980s chart band.

A few doors away was a red band called Steve who was a former soldier in the Army Intelligence Corps. Red bands are trustee prisoners who had extra privileges, and were all housed on 'C' wing. One of the best jobs in the prison that red bands could do was working in the officer's mess. I couldn't get over how different 'C' wing was and the prisoners were compared to the others, but like Castington, this privileged environment nauseated me too. I always hated to see grovelling and 'sucking up'. I preferred to be with the majority where we were all in the same boat. I didn't ask to go on 'C' wing.

I took up my education classes from where I'd left off and started studying English language towards my first ever exam. The teachers who worked at the prison were always very approachable and easy going, but it was common to get schoolboy crushes on some of them. After being deprived of female company for so long, it's easy to cling on to anything that touches the heart. It is very false though, as is the whole prison environment. It's all in the mind, but it can bring out the more sensitive side of a man. One of my fellow prisoners did have an affair with a teacher and the last I heard, they got married on his release. The interaction between us and the teachers made prison life a lot easier. We spent most of our days with them, and so we developed a good rapport and bond. They made us feel like human beings by calling us by our first names, or Mr ....

This familiarity was disapproved of by some of the screws who objected to this level of respect from them towards us. Thankfully, our liberal thinking teachers had their own way of doing things. And it was always a nice little victory to get one over on the screws. Also for me this was a huge turn around from my years of despising education and teachers. Prison education was my first encounter with academic work since I had walked out of my school exams five years before.

And here I was in prison and exam day arrived. The cell door suddenly opened where a screw stood with one of the teachers called Debbie. I was then led to an empty cell on the 'ones' to sit my test. I flew through the questions in the hour I was given, but I still had to wait a while until I was unlocked. Later, I felt as though I'd achieved something for the first time in my life, so I went back to my cell and lay down on my bed to reflect.

I had actually passed my first ever exam and it was from prison. I gained an RSA English language qualification. My results arrived after I'd been released and made my mother very proud. She used to tell me how when she used to leave the prison after visiting me, she'd see students sat in their classrooms at Durham University and wished I was one them instead of sitting in prison.

Although I was pleased with myself for my latest achievement, things were about to spoil it all. The governor had mentioned to me when I was recalled back to prison that I would be released on licence again, so I was so chuffed that I was getting out four weeks early. The day before I was to be released on licence again, I was taken down to reception to check my property, so this confirmed in my mind that I was going home again.

I was then taken to the wing office to see the P.O. where I was told they'd made a mistake and that I wasn't being released after all. He apologised and although I only had four weeks left to do, it had a bad effect on me psychologically because I had built my hopes up. So high were my feelings of anxiety, I remember while I was eating my lunch that afternoon, my nose suddenly started to bleed into my soup.

I was fed up with cockroaches in the cell, I didn't get on with my cellmate who I thought was a bit of a dope, and I had just had a nasty shock, so I wasn't in the best of moods. But it wasn't for long - after all - it was only four weeks away and that's what kept me going.

As the weeks passed, I was getting gate-happy again, and then finally, my earliest date of release (EDR) arrived. This was the release date where the sentence ended permanently (albeit with remission off for good behaviour). I had about an extra week to serve of lost remission which was added after I threw part of my table through the bars of my cell on to the grass at Castington and for my attempted escape. I was lucky here because they merely took remission from me for damaging property to the cell wall rather than attempting to escape.

Apart from that, a third of my sentence was taken off for good behaviour which was ten months. This meant I was to serve a total of twenty months - six of which I served on parole licence and fourteen inside. Your EDR is unlike parole where you're technically serving your sentence in the community and can be sent back to prison anytime - as I was. Your latest date of release (LDR) is when you've lost all you're remission for getting into trouble and you serve the full amount. For example, you end up serving the full five years of a five year sentence.

Some prisoners refused parole for this very reason, preferring to complete their sentences inside. Some felt that the controlling aspect of parole on their lives wasn't worth the stress. At least once you've completed your sentence, you didn't have to be supervised or abide by any rules set down by the Home Office or attend weekly appointments with a probation officer.

CHAPTER TWELVE

MAKING A FRESH START

Back home in Middlesbrough, I was leading a fairly stable lifestyle now. I was keen on fitness and weight-training going to Eston Sports Hall several times a week and running. I remember when I was first released from prison being too weak to run. It took several weeks of my mother's home-cooking to get me back to normal. But not long after, I started getting restless and got some crazy idea to go travelling around the country. I was looking for something but never knew what.

All I knew was, I couldn't settle in Teesside. So I set off for Birmingham and managed to find a hostel called *the Boot* in Digbeth to stay. *The Boot* was for homeless people. It had a reception area leading to a television room, and then a dormitory with about thirty beds.

As I got to know people, I discovered there was a group of 'rent boys' there and each night they would go and sell their 'wares' to the highest bidder. There was also a certain amount of intimidation towards younger residents who were encouraged to join them. And one night, one of them was coerced into having sex with two men in a car.

After that, he would wake up in the middle of the night screaming and crying. One of the rent boys used to meet a Catholic Priest each night outside *the Boot* where they would then go off somewhere. It was all very seedy and not the kind of environment I wanted to be in. The staff that ran *the Boot* were a great bunch of well-meaning people who helped me find somewhere more permanent to live. It was in a place called Hockley which wasn't far from Handsworth - notorious for riots and its high crime rate. During my time in Birmingham I associated with the seedier side of life. One of the lads from the hostel introduced me to his mates at a twenty-four hour café in Digbeth run by two gays. And late at night it would be full of transsexual men who used it as a late night 'stop off' in between soliciting themselves on the streets. Most nights there would be a fight between some of them over disputes or just pure jealousy because one had got more punters than the other, or encroached on another's patch.

Every day, I would go to a gay bar called *Legends*. It was full of interesting characters. I can remember it was next to a cinema which at the time was showing 'Rocky IV'. I didn't get much sleep in the hostel with all its comings and goings and I can recall always trying to keep myself awake during day time while sitting in *Legends*. I wasn't gay, I just liked the atmosphere such bars had.

Birmingham was a scary place for me back then and very much a multi-cultural society. This was all new to me. On Teesside, there was never a huge multi-cultural presence, so I found it extremely intimidating as I'd heard so much about racist violence here. One night in Hockley outside my bedroom window, a black pimp beat up a prostitute, while in Handsworth on another occasion, someone was blasted with a shotgun in a café.

It was a hotbed of criminal activity. I was seeing first hand, the effects the country's recession was having on different societies from the North-East to the Midlands and later, further afield. I had left Teesside where I witnessed the declining steel industry and all the effects it had on local people, and now in Birmingham, I was witnessing racial violence fuelled by social deprivation and police harassment. I could feel the tension around me like a pressure cooker about to explode. I had sensed these feelings before in prison.

When I moved into my new bedsit in Hockley, I was awarded Housing Benefit from the local council, but as soon as I received the cheque which included four weeks arrears, I cashed it and went on a boozing spree. Obviously, I knew this would catch up with me eventually, but rarely did I ever think of consequences. I couldn't cash it at a Post Office because it was addressed to the landlord, so I asked Billy who I had met at *the Boot* and who had a lot of contacts, if he knew a way I could get it cashed. He took me to a very shifty café and as we approached it, a black man standing just outside asked if we wanted to buy some drugs which we abruptly refused. We walked into the café when I was introduced to the Chinese owner who examined the cheque and after negotiating his percentage, cashed it for me. Of course my landlord at the bedsit finally got wind of my shenanigans and asked me to leave which I did and so I returned to Middlesbrough.

Once I was back home, I tried to lead as much of a normal life as possible - whatever that may be, but something would always spoil it. I was twenty-one, had no qualifications thanks to my disastrous schooling, had been dishonourably discharged from the army, had a criminal record, and a history of clinical depression. So there weren't many options open to me at the time.

I thought to myself that if I was to find work, I had to focus on jobs where I wouldn't be asked if I had a criminal record. I was feeling hyper-active now and ready to enjoy life and 'take the bull by the horns'. I was super fit and raring to find something to stimulate me. But the one thing that was always missing in my life was the love of a good woman. I always imagined a perfect life of myself going home to my wife and kids each night. I had an idealistic image of the perfect home life I wanted, with the two-point-five children and going home every night to a loving wife. But it was never to be.

Since my parent's divorce, rejection was a difficult pill to swallow. And once I started dating girls, splitting up became something I struggled to deal with. Although I knew it was part of life, I used to take it much harder than normal. I would get it real bad when I fell for someone, I was too 'full-on' and 'too serious'. Then when things went wrong, I always turned to my crutch which was alcohol, - the very thing that would drive me deeper into the depths of despair and anxiety. I was always restless and looking for something or someone to make me happy. I couldn't understand why I couldn't just lead a steady life like those around me. I remember always feeling desperately lonely, like there was a massive hole in my life, so much so, that I could feel it in the pit of my stomach. I had a permanent heartache and feelings of despair. I would often feel quite weepy and want to burst into tears.

I was very clingy to anyone who showed me even the slightest sign of affection or attention and would try to turn it into something much more. I used to become infatuated by girls I liked, believing there was more in it than there was. I had massive insecurities and feelings of emptiness. I always saw my relationships with women as something much bigger than was actually true.

I was like this from as far back as I could remember. I never had a normal love life with a regular girlfriend. I always attracted women however and always the ones who didn't want commitment, who had been in a bad marriage or relationship and who just wanted me when it was convenient for them. I used to attract women who were fascinated by my chequered past and spontaneity – women who had led dull lives and found being with me more exciting. But with no desire to settle down with me.

I attracted ones who had lots of baggage and problems with personal issues, who were able to connect with me because we had so much in common. They always said I needed mothering. For some reason I was like a magnet to women like this and it was a recipe for disaster.

I always yearned for stability and that family life that was taken from me as a boy. I had set ideas in my mind of the perfect family. It was my romanticism of a perfect life. My mood swings were unpredictable and the slightest rejection from a girl I liked would be enough to send me into a deep depression fuelled by alcohol. Rejection was something I couldn't handle. I had been rejected by my father, my teachers and peers, by girls and I had no emotional strength whatsoever. The only self esteem I built up was through working in the gym to build the perfect physique. I was a real gym freak and over the years had trained hard to get that muscular frame. On the outside I was seen as a powerful man who had endured all sorts of hardships in life, someone who could take care of women and protect them.

Women always foolishly thought that because on the outside I looked tough with a large muscular physique who acted quite confident, that inside I was the same. But it couldn't have been further from the truth and this was the problem. Inside I was an emotional wreck incapable of having a real relationship. At first the initial part of the romance was always exciting and passionate where we couldn't get enough of one another, but as fast as my so-called relationships began, they fizzled out. Once they could see how unstable and clingy I was, they soon lost interest and then I would desperately try to fix it and be the strong man they wanted. But I wasn't, I was weak and vulnerable and they didn't need another child as many told me over the years. They wanted a man. This just made me feel even more inadequate.

I had spent some time unemployed 'signing-on' at Hadrian House Social Security building in Eston once every two weeks, while in the meantime, job hunting. But most of my days were spent keeping fit. I was a real fitness freak. I appreciated the benefits of health and fitness more now and the stimulus that exercise can have on a person's well-being. Although I had been running and lifting weights since I was fifteen, I never really understood the psychological benefits exercise can have on a person until I was in my early twenties. I had just experienced the lows and frustrations of being incarcerated for months at a time. So running not only released the endorphins that give you that 'feel good' factor, but it gave me the ultimate appreciation of being free.

And I would often run at 2:00am when no one else was around, when the streets were quiet and the air was fresh. I reached a good level of fitness and was running eight to ten miles most days. I was keen on weight-training too and I'd been doing a lot in prison where I'd put quite a bit of muscle on. I also took up karate and kung fu and I seemed to have started leading a fairly stable life. I wasn't hammering the booze as before and I was enjoying my new athletic and healthier lifestyle.

I made the most of my spare time while I was unemployed. But *Giro* pay day was the highlight of every fortnight for everyone. The post office queues spilled out on to the pavement as everyone crammed in to cash their benefits. You could guarantee the pubs would be busy that day too and a good old session on the beer would follow. I amazed myself at one stage by actually giving up alcohol for six weeks. This was a miracle for me, but it also showed there was some sort of change coming over me and I did have strength of character after all. I kept my mind stimulated by going to *Redcar college* to study for an 'O' level in psychology which I really enjoyed doing. Since passing a basic English language exam in Durham prison, I felt I was able to take my education further and I'd always had an interest in psychology anyway.

I also enrolled on a fitness instructor course and one day the class spent the afternoon at *Redcar Leisure Centre* playing badminton. Well, at least the others did. I went in the weights room. I'd over trained that day which I often did. It was a hot day and I recall running around the college field in the afternoon then training on the weights and now here I was again training even more. It can become as addictive as other things can, but for me it was so addictive because of that 'feel good factor'.

One of the female students had taken a shine to me which was a great boost to my confidence. I hadn't been out of prison long and I was feeling a bit self-conscious. She sat and watched me train until it was time to go back to the college. After college ended, I headed into Redcar High Street when I saw the same young girl sat with a skinhead with tattoos round his throat with his arm around her.

He gave me a sort of smirk, but not thinking anything of it I carried on walking and stood in the bus queue for grangetown. I then felt a tap on my right shoulder and saw the skinhead standing there who started to warn me what would happen to me if I didn't leave his girlfriend alone. She wasn't his girlfriend; he was just being a pest. Not having any patience with idiots like this and having just spent over a year locked up with hundreds of them, I threw a punch which he managed to avoid. And then it turned into a full-blown street fight right outside the *Clarendon Hotel*.

As the skinny 'yob' attempted a rather pathetic karate kick, I managed to grab him and hurl him to the ground where I then kneeled across him and squeezed his throat. As a typical coward though, he put his hands up and begged me not to hit him. As I said before, the bully is always a coward. Another skinhead then appeared who tried to intimidate me by saying, 'Did you say you something about Redcar skins?' I said 'no'! - while thinking how pathetic they were. I would have smacked that idiot too had they not disappeared. Gangs always made me laugh, because it just highlights their total insecurities as men.

Although I was enjoying my athletic lifestyle and new zest for education, I desperately needed work. I thought about touring the country again to find work. Then around this time, my mother's brother, Donald, started to become a big part of our lives. He was having a tough time, because over the course of one week, he had to retire, which meant he had to give up his house as it went with the job. And tragically, his beloved wife of thirty years, Mary, unexpectedly died of cancer.

When he came into our lives, things changed for us forever. He was one of the most intelligent men I had ever met. He had three degrees and two diplomas. His career spanned fifty years during which time he had gained the Fellowship of the *Royal Anthropological Institute* for his research done on the Veda tribe of Ceylon, now Sri Lanka. He had worked for Barnado's as a child psychologist for gifted and disturbed children, was an accomplished writer, writing hundreds of articles for the *Salisbury Medical Journal*, reported for the *Salisbury*

Journal newspaper and had also worked for the *Salisbury Western Gazette.*

He achieved degrees in law, anatomy and physiology, a diploma in psychology and finally a postgraduate medical history diploma at London University when he was sixty-six years old. It was his thirst for knowledge and continual educational achievements that inspired me most of all. I was still struggling to find a job with no skills or qualifications. So, one day, Donald thought it would be a good idea for me to go back with him to Salisbury to try and find work. I could never go for the sort of job I really wanted, because of my criminal convictions, lack of qualifications and no work history.

So I always applied for jobs where I could get a quick start and where they wouldn't delve into my past. And it was the catering industry that provided this opportunity. I soon realised that the catering industry had a high turnover of staff, but you could always land a job somewhere, often with accommodation thrown in, including meals and more than often, with an immediate start.

It was also an industry that took you on at face value and gave people a chance. And as I discovered later, recognised experience as being more important than qualifications. It was my chance to build a career for myself and leave the past behind. I had my own independence, job security and pride. My only problem was, I never stayed in a job long enough to build a stable work history. I soon got tired of the long daily grind, and then I would start looking for somewhere else to work. Mostly though, it was because of the volatile temperament of the catering staff. However, Salisbury is where my working life began for me. The South was a huge culture change and I was looking forward to the new challenges. I shared a flat with Donald and we got along quite well despite the age gap. He was sixty-six and I was twenty-three, but we were good mates and we regularly went to the pub together. We had some great times and he was as energetic as anyone I knew.

He had a real zest for life. He was a well respected member of the community and since retiring from the *Salisbury Journal*, they had decided to keep him on working part-time writing his regular history column called *Curious Salisbury* and covering the weekly court reports. In those days, the editorial staff would meet at the pub for a liquid lunch each day. The pub was an extension of the newsroom and a culture which has since long gone. He was always active, he couldn't give up work. I got to meet his circle of friends who included local solicitors, councillors, police officers and even a high court judge once.

During my time here I met the *Only Fools and Horses* sitcom cast who had come to stay for a week to visit patients at the local spinal unit. I spoke to David Jason and Nicholas Lyndhurst and the hotel where they were staying which was usually very quiet was packed in the bar every night for that week.

Salisbury was a quaint little town and was a huge change from back home. Unemployment was a lot lower and the dole queues were barely visible. I could see that everyone had a job and it was refreshing to find that there were jobs to be had - a complete contrast to my home in Middlesbrough. I enjoyed the prospects the south offered me. It had opportunities that I was looking forward to exploring. There was a buzz about the place and every morning the town was busy with people going to work and about their business. Back home on Teesside there were some days when you wouldn't see a single soul all day. Others on Teesside followed suit and moved away from Teesside to find work - it seemed to be the only way.

I was still hanging around though without any real purpose in life, then, one day, Donald suggested I visit some hotels to enquire about job vacancies. It sounded easier than I expected. But I decided to give it a go, so I went out one night for a few drinks when I came across the *County Hotel*. I made a casual enquiry at the bar and straight away was taken to see the duty manager who offered me a job on the spot working as a KP (kitchen porter).

This was basically washing up, keeping the kitchen clean and tidy and general dogs-bodying. In many ways, the catering industry suited me because it allowed me to travel around the UK and Europe experiencing different places. And though I hated the temperamental environment that went along with the catering industry, I have to say I had some great times too. Hotels had their own unique culture as did all the institutions such as the army, prison, hospitals and hotels. Whichever hotel I worked in, I could see the same types of characters in every hotel.

Prison was the same. Whichever prison you go to, you come across the same culture but just different people who talk and act the same way. I saw the same in the army where many of the soldiers spoke and behaved the same. While living in the south, there were things I missed from the north and it's strange how you miss the smallest things that you would never think about normally. While having my lunch at the *White Horse Hotel* bar where my uncle and his workmates from the Journal hung out every afternoon, I ordered apple pie and custard - to the surprise of the barperson who replied, 'Oh we don't serve custard down here, we serve cream'. Fish and chip shops didn't have mushy peas and the pubs never served lager with a frothy head on.

I was still running a lot and using weights, but even the gymnasiums were more up-market. I couldn't find a real weight training room like the ones I was used to go to back home with clanking barbells and dumbells. At work, the long shift patterns, split shifts and weekend work that goes with the catering trade was not for me.

But I loved the bond I had with my fellow workmates. It was like being part of a big family. We spent more time working with one another than with our own relatives. The hotel life provided me with an extended family which is what I loved about the catering industry most of all.

This came from an underlying need to be part of group of people who all worked closely to one another. They were like a family spending long periods of time working together, developing close relationships. Despite the long hours, I thrived on routine at first and for this part of the work, it was perfect. The catering industry brought out all the positives and negatives of my life.

There was the sense of belonging and having close friends, of being part of a social group and a uniformed brigade of chefs, but it wasn't the right place for me to be and my drinking became worse. I thought I had found my niche in life. I had a regular wage, a great social life and I was aware that some of the girls I worked with were interested in me. But I felt as though I was missing out on something else.

I remember one day during a quiet period at work picking up a newspaper and being shocked at the headlines about a child abuse scandal in Cleveland. I was horrified to read that was happening in my hometown, but even more horrified that innocent people were being accused of child abuse, a common occurrence nowadays.

Then as I opened the centre pages, I recognised someone who I was at school with. His was the first family caught up in the fiasco. The whole nightmare compared to the Salem witch-trials 300 years before by Middlesbrough MP Stuart Bell, saw 121 cases of children taken from their parents. Such was the horror of it all, one father had a heart attack and one lady had an abortion so as not to have her child taken from her.

There was an arson attack on one home, windows smashed, one family evacuated, while fathers, grandfathers and neighbours were falsely accused. Tension created near riots with children being taken away without notice sometimes in the middle of the night from families, and from schools and communities. There were conflicts between *Cleveland Police, Cleveland Social Services* and the *North Regional Health Authority*. There was a national outcry, national debate, statements on the floor of the House of Commons and a judicial enquiry which was to be the longest in British history. And this was all happening back home in Teesside.

In retrospect of the Cleveland crisis, one would hope that all the failings of society and professional bodies would have brought major changes in attitudes over child abuse allegations. Yet it has been demonstrated time again how easy it is for someone to be falsely accused, for the accused to be condemned to a life of misery and labelling, while the accusers walk free unscathed. Child abuse allegations are the witch-trials of modern society, with false allegations used as an excuse for vendettas and witch-hunts in the form of vigilantism.

During my time in Salisbury, I'd had several bad episodes of mood swings and bouts of depression that became more and more regular. But there were deeper problems behind my inability to focus and settle. Serious personality changes were starting to come to the fore. Already I had committed offences and done time, but something deeper and more sinister was beginning to happen to me. I started to get more frequent depressions for little reason. I can remember feeling unbearably dysfunctional at times. It was as though a dark cloud was passing over me - but for no reason.

Something biological was changing inside me which would make me incapable of leading a normal life at times. I can't express the level of despair I was starting to feel, but it was extremely debilitating at times. Donald had a few contacts in the medical profession and arranged for me to see one the countries top psychiatrists who at first diagnosed me as a paranoid schizophrenic.

But later put it down to me being deeply, emotionally disturbed. I had occasional episodes of meaningless, angry outbursts and I knew something wasn't right. This is where alcohol now became a sedative rather than a social pastime. I had been drinking too much anyway but I was still a fitness fanatic. I'd had several bad episodes of mood swings, feelings of huge despair and depression that became more and more regular. But nobody could help me or tell me what was happening to me.

When I was working in Salisbury, Donald had persuaded me to be committed to *The Old Manor* psychiatric hospital for assessment. I hadn't been in there an hour when a paranoid patient threatened me, so I left after a heated debate with the doctor who tried to keep me in. It was a place nightmares were made of. I didn't much like the staff either. But unfortunately for me, it was a missed opportunity on being given an essential diagnosis.

Despite my problems, I was soon to find myself becoming part of something that would give me a real purpose in life and help me psychologically.

CHAPTER THIRTEEN

WHEN I DARED AND ALMOST WON

While I was living in Salisbury, an opportunity arose for me to set things straight with the army and at the same time experience the excitement from army Infantry training I'd been denied by the RAOC six years earlier. It would also be my way of giving something back to the army as well as getting something from it myself. I had never really forgiven myself for messing up my short-lived army career, so I was always looking for an opportunity to put this right and here was that opportunity. One day in 1987 while I was walking along Castle Street in Salisbury, I saw a sign in the army careers office window. The sign read something along the lines of - *Territorial Army 21st SAS Regiment - Applicants Wanted - Enquire Within.*

A simple sign I thought for such a reputable regiment. I didn't even know they had a TA unit. I went in to enquire about it where I was met by the recruitment sergeant who asked, 'How many miles do you run a day'? to which I replied, 'I run eight miles, about four times a week.' He then answered, 'Well when you've been doing that every day for about a year with a pack on your back, come back and ask again.'

I left feeling deflated but plucked up the courage to go back a few days later and ask again. This time someone different was at the desk who was more accommodating than the last person, so I got my application in. Several weeks passed when a letter arrived inviting me for an interview to a place called Bramley near Basingstoke. I was excited by this, but I always had a nagging worry in the back of my mind that one day they would discover my criminal record. I didn't reveal my criminal history as it had become the 'norm' to lie on application forms if I was ever to get anywhere in life. I had no intention of doing anything wrong or breaking the law, yet I was breaking the law by not disclosing my convictions on application forms.

Several years earlier I had applied to join the 23rd (TA) SAS Regiment in Prudhoe, Northumberland where I was honest about my criminal record, but rejected because of it. So after numerous failed attempts to join the honest way, I decided not to disclose my convictions anymore. And that went for both the TA, and for jobs. I'd had enough of continual rejection. Neither did I reveal that I had once been in the regular army. So naturally, I was amazed when I was accepted. Of course this was the early computer age, so records were not as efficient as they are now.

However, despite expecting to be tapped on the shoulder any day and chucked out, I carried on turning up every Wednesday night for training. Here we would practice map reading, drill, weapons training and some fitness. I was in awe of the instructors, many of whom were regular SAS soldiers from 22 regiment. I don't know what I'd expected to see heading to camp for the first time, but they were all quite ordinary to look at, mostly of small stocky stature.

SAS selection is reported to be the most demanding military training course in the British Armed Forces with a reported pass rate of less than ten-per-cent. It is a test of strength, endurance, and resolve over the Brecon Beacons and Elan Valley in Wales. Our initial pre-selection test

Top left: Me aged 10, 1973
Top right: Carol aged 7, me aged 2, 1965
Bottom left: My passing out parade day, 1981
Bottom right: Mam and me in the garden of my digs in Haxby road, York, 1988

Top: Infamous Durham prison
Bottom: A prisoner slopping out

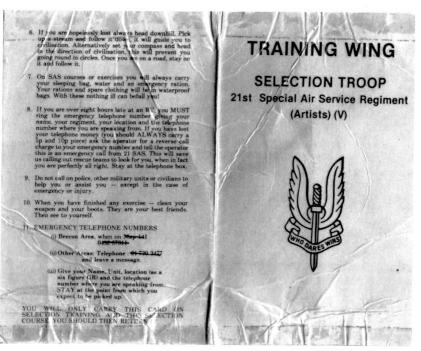

6. If you are hopelessly lost always head downhill. Pick up a stream and follow it down, it will guide you to civilisation. Alternatively set your compass and head in the direction of civilisation, this will prevent you going round in circles. Once you are on a road, stay on it and follow it.

7. On SAS courses or exercises you will always carry your sleeping bag, water and an emergency ration. Your rations and spare clothing will be in waterproof bags. With these nothing ill can befall you!

8. If you are over eight hours late at an RV, you MUST ring the emergency telephone number giving your name, your regiment, your location and the telephone number where you are speaking from. If you have lost your telephone money (you should ALWAYS carry a 5p and 10p piece) ask the operator for a reverse call charge to your emergency number and tell the operator this is an emergency call from 21 SAS. This will save us calling out rescue teams to look for you, when in fact you are perfectly all right. Stay at the telephone box.

9. Do not call on police, other military units or civilians to help you or assist you — except in the case of emergency or injury.

10. When you have finished any exercise — clean your weapon and your boots. They are your best friends. Then see to yourself.

11. EMERGENCY TELEPHONE NUMBERS

   (i) Brecon Area, when on Map 141
      0492-57011

   (ii) Other Areas: Telephone : 01-730 3477
      and leave a message.

   (iii) Give your Name, Unit, location (as a six figure GR) and the telephone number where you are speaking from. STAY at the point from which you expect to be picked up.

YOU WILL ONLY CARRY THIS CARD ON SELECTION TRAINING AND THE SELECTION COURSE. YOU SHOULD THEN RETURN IT.

TRAINING WING

SELECTION TROOP
21st Special Air Service Regiment
(Artists) (V)

WHO DARES WINS

Top: SAS recruits yomping/tabbing over misty Brecon.
Bottom: My SAS identity/survival drill card.

REG KRAY ✦ 30 YEARS ✦ 1968-1998

HMP WAYLAND, C-WING, GRISTON, THETFORD, NORFOLK IP25 6RL

"Life is not a rehearsal …
so make the most of it."

Books written by Reg Kray

Title	Published by
Born Fighter	Century
Our Story	Sidgwick & Jackson Ltd
Slang	Sidgwick & Jackson Ltd
Villains We Have Known	Arrow Books
Thoughts	Soon to be republished
Epilogue of Ron Kray	*Video - produced by Reg Kray. Write to PO Box 56, Watton, Norfolk IP25 6JY*

<u>Reg Kray's internet site</u> is: **http://www.room102.co.uk/kraytwins**

Top: Signed note from Reg Kray for my part in the campaign.
Bottom left: Signed photo from Reg Kray (right of picture).
Bottom right: Myself with 'Mad' Frank Fraser at his book
signing in Newcastle, 1998.

Prison education gives a degree of freedom

David was determined to break free from prison. But he chose education as his escape. He told IAN MARLAND his tale.

Knowledge is the key: David about to begin a degree course at Northumbria University, found his third spell in jail was a turning point.

Top: Newcastle Journal article, 1998.
Bottom: Donald me and mam on my first graduation day, 2001.
The last photo I had with Donald.

Graduation day for my master's degree in 2003.

took place at Hereford where the regular SAS were based. We spent the weekend in an aircraft hanger where we were issued sleeping bags. As the coach slowly drove into the camp, I remember seeing a disused passenger aeroplane where the anti-terrorist unit practiced their rescue drills. This really excited me and reminded me of the Iranian Embassy siege in London in 1980. As we settled in, we were given a talk by the Commanding Officer about how much fitness we had to do and the self discipline that was required from us.

We were told to keep a fitness diary of everything we did; something I have continued to do to this day. There were several tests before we could be fully accepted into the regiment as troopers. The first was an eight mile run as a group. I had no problem with this expect I wore plimsolls and developed a black toenail for my trouble. The most memorable test was when we were all ordered to strip naked and plunge into a pond with a temperature of five above freezing. This was testing our resistance to hypothermia. It was 100 yards swim and as soon as I hit the water, every bit of my energy left me. I remember feeling that only 'mind over matter' could get me to the other side.

I had superb fitness and was now a strong swimmer, unlike eight years earlier when I almost drown during my 'regular army' swimming test. After that ordeal, I went to Eston swimming baths everyday once I'd been kicked out of the army. I taught myself to tread water and swim stronger until I had no fear of any water no matter how deep, whatsoever. But here I was fighting against sheer freezing temperatures.

I just kept putting one arm in front of the other until I reached the other side. Climbing on to the muddy bank I looked across and saw that one man was being helped into a sleeping bag with another man as he had suffered hypothermia from the freezing cold water. The instructors were laughing at how our 'wedding tackle' had shrivelled up with the coldness. The SAS instructors were not as bothered with bull-shit as the usual army instructors were. I had read this many years ago in a book called *Who Dares Wins.* There's no screaming at you all the time or the usual obsession with polishing and standing to attention every time you spoke to a senior rank.

There's no saluting in the SAS as you go about your daily business, and there's no, 'Yes Sir, 'No Sir', Three bags full sir'. You call officers, 'Boss'. The SAS regiment is more interested in your soldiering skills than how shiny your boots are, or if you have razor sharp creases in your trousers. They want to know if you can survive extremities and if they can trust you with their lives.

The next test was potholing which consisted of us being taken in groups and sent down drains where we crawled through dark tunnels. You could only go one way as it was too narrow to turn yourself around. We had to find our way out and while we were in there, they started to fill the tunnels with water, so the faster we got out, the better. This was to test our reaction to claustrophobia.

The final test was an assault course which I had a problem with at first. Every time I attempted the monkey bars which are overhead iron bars you hang from and pull yourself forward, my hands slipped and I couldn't get across. After several unsuccessful attempts, the sergeant shouted, 'Okay Honeywell, last go!'

With every bit of concentration I could conjure up, I leapt on to the bars and moved as fast as I could grasping each bar as tight as I could, moving forward clearing the whole obstacle. Once the assault course was completed, I knew I had passed the weekend. Quietly satisfied, we all travelled back to base that Sunday afternoon where we were debriefed and then dismissed. I then headed back to Salisbury where Donald met me at the train station.

I was full of it, excited at the prospect of being selected for SAS training. Several days passed when I received my acceptance letter telling me to report to Bramley army base each Wednesday night with the programme for the forthcoming gruelling six months that ended with a forty mile 'yomp' over Brecon Beacons. Yomp is Royal Marines slang describing a long-distance march carrying full kit. We also called it 'tabbing' which means, 'Tactical Advance to Battle'. In many ways it was harder living the life as a reservist because you had go back to normal living on Monday morning as you would if you'd just spent the weekend camping or fishing.

Our base in Bramley was in the middle of nowhere so I walked the distance from the town to camp. I was always there first so I'd go for a run around the nearby woods for an hour before the others turned up. At the end of each night, we would congregate in the bar and socialise. I was chatting to a major one night at the bar because as I said, there was no rank distinction in the regiment outside training. I asked him if we would be learning any unarmed combat training. As he leaned on the bar, he picked up a very solid looking glass ashtray and said in his perfectly clear cut English accent, 'Well all you need to do is, pick up the nearest heaviest object and smash them across the head with it.' I never did do that; I decided to continue martial arts training instead.

During our long distance marches we had to achieve a certain distance, within a certain time, carrying varying amounts of weight in our bergens. The directing staff was there to assess us and set the times of the marches. The training instructors knew in a short time what kind of people we were. The selection process is very good at identifying that area of a person's build-up. Our squadron NCO, Corporal Reid got myself and two others to one side on Brecon and told us we had exactly what it takes and really wanted us get through. Weekend training was always either on Brecon Beacons or the Black Mountains which involved slogging over the mountains in wet and freezing conditions.

Everything was packed in our bergens in a certain way to distribute the weight evenly on our backs. The heaviest items always went at the bottom and the lightest at the top. Then to support our lower back, we inserted a foam sleeping mat (roll mat) into the lower part of the bergen.

The roll mats were actually to go underneath our sleeping bags when we were asleep. We used to cut them in half so they would fit into the bergens. The weight in the bergen is initially made up of essential items that consists of foul-weather gear, a sleeping bag, medical equipment and distress flares. The food carried is your ration for the day which generally consists of bread rolls, probably a couple Mars bars, and crisps; in addition a candidate will carry a normal army twenty-four-hour ration pack which can only be opened in an emergency.

The first night we camped out on Brecon, I managed to let all the rain seep in so I woke up the next morning soaked in a drenched sleeping bag and freezing cold. The idea was to use our ponchos as cover by tying each corner to a tree or securing them to other things if there were no trees anywhere. But you should always test the ground to make sure it's all even where you're lying down, otherwise should it rain, it will seep underneath you and soak you. I learned this the hard way. We were told that we always had to have a set of dry clothes in our bergens which we could wear while we were asleep. But the next morning, we had to pack these dry clothes back into our bergens and put our wet clothes from the day before back on. They were permanently soaked from each days marching. It wasn't pleasant at 5.30am in the freezing cold, but it was the only way to ensure you always had a dry set of clothes ready for the next night.

But because I'd managed to soak myself and my sleeping bag, the rest of the weekend was very uncomfortable. I had no dry clothes at all to sleep in. I was uncontrollably shivering the next morning and eager to get walking again so I could warm my body heat up. The marches started Friday nights, lasted all day and all night on Saturday and part of Sunday morning. I always struggled to keep up with the others because the soles of my feet used to burn so much. I was one of the fittest when it came to running, but yomping over hilly mountains and acres of moon grass was a different story.

A medical officer took a look at my blistered feet at one of the rendezvous after I told him of the burning sensation I felt. He explained that I had fallen arches and therefore I would feel it more, and that I needed to buy some insoles that could create an arch for more comfort. Some of the others were starting to bring their own things for comfort each weekend. I noticed some had waterproof covers for their sleeping bags and some brought their own food to add to their rations. Some carried those Rambo knives that were all the craze then since the film *First Blood* and its sequels became popular.

One morning when we were lined up waiting for inspection, we were laid into by the main instructor. He got us all to empty our bergens so everything was displayed in front of us. Foaming at the mouth, he ripped into us, 'You're supposed to be training to be SAS soldiers. 'This isn't real life he said', holding up someone's *Rambo* knife. There were many times we risked life and limb on the mountains and one person did tragically lose his life when he fell from a mountain on Brecon. Our instructor held on to him for dear life until he just couldn't hold on anymore. This was chilling but I had no idea I would almost meet the same fate.

During the first selection I got hypothermia and on the second attempt, I got heat exhaustion. My first near disaster happened when we had to do what is known as the 'Fan dance'. 'The Fan Dance' is a 25km route march and one of the British Army's most gruelling physical tests. Originally devised as a part of the initial training for the Parachute Regiment's Battle School, the 'Fan Dance' is now a test run by the Infantry Battle School, as a mandatory part of the training and selection for Section Commanders, Platoon Sergeants and Platoon Commanders throughout the Infantry. 'The Fan Dance' also forms part of the selection course for UK Special Forces.

The SAS always work in teams of four. I was with three others as we set off to do the 'Fan Dance', when I lost sight of my team and became lost in a mist at the highest peak of Brecon, known as *Pen Y Fan*. I was trapped with no visibility whatsoever at 886 metres (2,907 feet) above sea-level, at the highest peak in Britain, south of the Snowdonia mountain range.

I walked around aimlessly and as my map reading skills weren't great, I ended up going missing. I started to come down with hypothermia and I remember seeing a fox but my vision was so blurred I didn't know if I was imagining things. I was shivering, disorientated and worried about the backlash I would get from the instructors. Although we were told never to fall asleep if we got hypothermia, I was exhausted so I got under my poncho and nodded off. My feet were badly blistered and my socks and boots were soaked. When I woke up, I took two carrier bags from my bergen and put them around my feet to keep them dry. Then I set off again and did what we were taught to do, by following a stream which leads to a river, which then leads to a road.

Two hours had passed from when I was supposed to report back to the rendezvous. I kept walking and tried to flag down a car. Several cars and lorries passed me, then eventually a car pulled over and a nice young couple gave me a lift just in time for me to reach base where a helicopter was setting off to go in search for me. Just as it hovered above, the instructors set flares off to alert the pilot I was safe.

It was now dark and they weren't amused. I was allowed to attempt another go at selection in the summer with the next intake, but this time the whole physical effort and the heat of the sun was all just too much for me. I remember half way through our yomp on Brecon; I ended up crawling on my hands and knees across some vast terrain as I just couldn't stand up anymore.

I had absolutely nothing left in me, all my energy had drained. But I got some comfort from the thirst quenching can of coke (*coca-cola)* hidden inside the bottom of my bergen. Earlier that week at Bramley, Cpl. Reid, had suggested I hide a can of coke at the bottom of my bergen and drink it when I became desperately thirsty.

The only thing was, before every march, our bergens were inspected to make sure we hadn't brought along any extra little luxuries, and also to make sure we had packed it correctly after which it was then weighed, to ensure we all had the same poundage on our backs. Cpl. Reid told me it would be him who would be doing the inspection the next time so it would be okay. Sure enough he inspected everyone's bergen that morning and turned a blind eye to the can of coke I had tucked inside the bottom, underneath the inner liner.

The liner was like a waterproof bag which kept everything dry from the merciless weather. Even during the summer, the weather on Brecon could take a nasty turn for the worse as many have discovered to their peril. I finally succumbed to the heat that day and sheer exhaustion of the endless yomping. Eventually, I was unable to walk, so crawling on my hands and knees; I found a spot to rest. I rummaged in my bergen for the coke, and as I gulped it down, it was like the elixir of life. And since then I have always had a thing about *coca-cola*.

I had joined with over a hundred others initially and by the time it was the end of the line for me, I had been part of the SAS selection process for a year. I had attempted it twice and ended up being one of the last six recruits before the pace got the better of me. I know another two failed selection that day which was on my twenty-third birthday, while the other three went on to become SAS soldiers. This had probably been one of the most stabilising periods of my life to date. I had discipline, a job, money and was able to leave the past behind for a while. At the same time I felt I had settled things with the army.

I had always looked forward to the weekends away and was very conscientious. I had become a recruit in the infamous SAS 'territorial' regiment. At least this time though, I wasn't sent home by the army for getting into trouble, it was because like hundreds before me, the SAS training was just beyond me. Nevertheless, this time I was able to hand over my kit with my head held high. I was gutted, but proud to have achieved what I had. I still took the rejection way too hard and depression hit again, but at least I tried.

CHAPTER FOURTEEN

GOING 'ROUND THE BEND'

I always managed to get jobs washing up in hotels, but never settled for long. I felt as though I was missing out on life - always being stuck in a kitchen day and night. I couldn't stay in one job for more than just a few weeks. The longest was for three months. I felt I would be better suited to a nine till five job where my evenings and weekends were my own.

I set off back to York in 1988 in search of employment. This was the first time I'd been back since my arrest in 1983. I worked at the *Dean Court Hotel* for a short while as a washer up which was a lot of fun as I remember. The staff were a good bunch of people and we all socialised outside of work together.

Then I started working as a doorman - firstly at the *Old Orleans,* which was a trendy sort of wine bar (now Tesco). I was the first to ever work on the doors there, alongside an Australian lad. I then got work at the *Railway King* in George Hudson Street, which at the time of me writing this, is called, *Reflex*. I always wanted to be part of the underworld and it was the doorman culture that provided this opportunity. It's more prevalent nowadays in places such as Newcastle and Sunderland but in 80s York, I couldn't see evidence of this. Later in life I met lots of my gangster colleagues through the doors. The only thing was, by the time this happened, I was unable to get a badge to work on doors due to my criminal convictions. Some of my old haunts I remembered from the early 80s had now closed down such as *the Pageant* just around the corner from the *Railway King* - a bar ran by several gays for all and sundry to enjoy. It was a real 'spit and sawdust' place, but so entertaining.

Each night the female staff would dance on top of the bar while the others lined up behind it banging tambourines to the sound of 60s hit, *The Legend of Xanadu by Dave Dee, Dozy, Beaky, Mick and Tich.* It had a real gritty fun atmosphere to it. Race days were the worst when mobs of gangs would descend on the City. You could guarantee there'd be trouble somewhere.

We didn't get much trouble in the *Railway King*. But there was always a bit of chew when we had to turn away groups because someone was wearing trainers or jeans. This was the dress code but it was always a bit dodgy as there was only two of us working on the door. Sometimes we'd have to face up to twenty drunk, boisterous men from out of town. And these were the days before CCTV.

I'd had trouble outside *Railway King* back in '83' when I was followed by a huge deaf and dumb guy. I was twenty at the time and as I was heading for the bar, he latched on to me and wouldn't leave me alone. Then he stood right in front of me not allowing past. He was at least six feet tall and of large build.

I knew I could be in real trouble here if I didn't do something, so I lashed out with a right punch to the rib cage and then one to the jaw. He hit the ground and slumped at the railings outside the doorway. I got away fast and headed off to another pub.

Sometimes you just don't have time to dither and risk getting a beating. Hit first, has always been my motto.

Another notorious watering hole in York was *Casanova's* nightclub which was eventually closed down by the licence courts. I worked there as a doorman too.

It was here I learned how to be ruthless with troublemakers because when trouble started, nobody cared who got hurt. One night a big fight kicked off and I ended up in the middle getting punched from all angles. Then at this point a fellow twenty-one stone doorman called Neil bear-hugged the ring leader and while grappling, they both fell on to a brass tube barrier which completely buckled under the weight.

I managed to get the culprits arm locked up his back at which point he was hurled out the front door. Neil later told me that we can't afford to hesitate. 'You have to stick your fingers in eyes, grab hair - whatever it takes' he said. I never entered a situation on my own again after that. You can always sense trouble brewing long before it starts and there are so many incidents I see today where violence could be 'nipped in the bud' long before it kicks off. I was training on the weights a lot and gaining some real size at this time.

I used to train at *Physical Wrecks* gym in Monkgate which was owned by Fred. There was a few characters used to get in the gym. Fred had a lot of experience training people and helped me a lot with training and advice. There were a lot of characters at the gym. One of the regulars was a local well known lad called Tony (Tote) Claridge. He had tremendous strength and although a reputation for being a hard man, was actually a real gentleman - always very polite and courteous. Another was Paul Garner who had the most amazing physique and had entered several major competitions. Fred and I became very good friends and not long after, a chef who Fred knew, found me a job as a kitchen porter at the *Crest hotel* now *(The Hilton York)* where he worked. Soon after starting there, I began dating a waitress called Denise, but it was complicated from the start.

Although I was now twenty-five, I had never had a serious girlfriend. My life had been too haywire, so I was still very inexperienced with matters of the heart. I know I had slept with a prostitute when I was in the army, but that was purely for the sexual experience. I believe my inexperience was behind a lot of my relationship problems over the years because I was a late starter. I went through emotions I had never felt before in my entire life. Denise and I first properly connected one day when I was sat in York Magistrates' Court awaiting my fate for defaulting on paying a fine for a criminal damage charge.

I was sat waiting in the corridor when she walked in. I thought how sexy she looked. I was used to seeing her at work in her waitress uniform. Today she wore a black two-piece outfit and high heels and looked a million dollars. She'd had some things stolen by her ex-boyfriend and was there to see if they'd been recovered.

She sat next to me chatting away and was curious about why I was there. I explained how one night I'd put a window through at the *Tam O' Shanter* pub, just for the hell of it. I went into detail about how I was walking past the pub one night when I got this insane urge to elbow one of their windows through.

This was another one of my most stupid ideas. I recalled how the regulars - including the landlord came running out of the pub and gave me a good kicking and how I then recovered myself and started attacking them.

Of course, when the police arrived, all they saw was me lashing out at them and completely missed them giving me a kicking. I was arrested that night at the scene of the crime and charged with criminal damage. I had deserved what I got though.

The landlord gave some 'cock and bull' story that the pub window was of a special make so they were more expensive than most. I was fined £300, but didn't keep up the payments, so here I was, hauled in front of the magistrates. I was ordered to continue paying instalments.

Denise was going through a trial separation with her husband, then one night, at the hotel's Christmas party which was held in January at the *Abbey Park hotel* on the Mount, we got together, had a dance and then spent the night together. Our relationship was very sexual as all my relationships were. But that night changed everything for me. The one thing that was always missing in my life was the love of a good woman.

Deluded though I was, I always imagined a perfect life of going home to a loving wife and kids each night. I had an idealistic image of the perfect home life I wanted, but it was never to be. Since my parent's divorce, rejection was a difficult pill to swallow. And once I started dating girls, splitting up became something I struggled to deal with. Although I knew it was part of life, I used to take it very hard.

Looking back, all my relationships were based on sex and as much and often as possible. I even remember a good friend having a quiet word with me because Denise had confided in his wife that I was too demanding. Apparently, three times a day was too excessive. I think I was just making up for lost time - or was highly sexed myself. Then again, Denise was highly sexed.

We would find anywhere and everywhere to have sex. I was always one for experimenting. We made love in horse stables where she worked, in the woods, in a shop doorway, in the back of her car. And had I just been satisfied with all this, I'm sure it would have carried on like that for years.

I was always looking for something deeper and more meaningful though - or someone to make me happy. But couldn't understand why I couldn't just lead a steady life like those seemingly happy couples around me. I remember always feeling desperately lonely, like there was a massive hole in my life, so much so, that I could feel it in the pit of my stomach.

I had massive insecurities and feelings of emptiness. I was like this from as far back as I could remember. I never had a steady girlfriend, just lots who didn't want commitment - who had been in bad marriages or relationships and who just wanted the excitement of an affair. The women I attracted were fascinated by my chequered past and spontaneity because they had led such dull lives and found being with me more exciting.

But they had no desire to settle down with me. They always had lots of baggage and problems with personal issues. Because of this, they were able to connect with me having had so much in common. For some reason I was like a magnet to women like this, but it was always a recipe for disaster.

At first the initial part of the romance was always exciting and passionate where we couldn't get enough of one another, but as fast as my so-called relationships began, they fizzled out. I couldn't handle the flirtatiousness either. Denise was very flirtatious and it caused a lot of arguments.

I was a desperately unhappy person and my depressions started to become so bad, that one night I took a razor and cut deep into my wrists - slashing them ten times. I woke the next morning surrounded by blood on the floor and all over my sheets. Yet somehow I managed to get myself ready and still go to work at *Physical Wrecks* where I'd been covering some shifts for Fred.

I felt so drowsy and drained of all energy. I later telephoned Fred and asked if he would come and see me.

As I unwrapped my bandaged wrists to show him what I'd done, he almost 'threw up'.

You could see the insides of my wrists where I'd hacked away. He took me straight to *York District Hospital* where I spent several days being stitched up and then assessed by the psychiatrist.

As my relationship with Denise developed, she left her husband and divorced him for me when we moved in together. We found a double room in a shared house in Scarcroft road. It was all too much upheaval for Denise. I knew she was getting itchy feet by the way she was talking and I started to become very possessive and totally paranoid that she was going to leave me.

She was unable to live with the fact that her kids were with her ex-husband and it understandably got to her. I was too immature to understand how much this must have affected her at the time. Denise was missing her kids and my suffocating presence got too much for her. Then one day, after an argument, I threw a hot frying pan from the oven ring against the kitchen wall.

At that point, Denise had taken as much as she could and walked out on me. About two days later when I came home one evening, I went upstairs to our bedroom and the first thing I saw, was an empty wardrobe. She'd packed and left while I was out. I started to turn things over in my mind, over and over again. I felt that others at the hotel had influenced her decision to do this. I know she kept in touch with her former work colleagues and I knew some of them disapproved of me. I felt that quite a few of her friends had it in for me. My paranoia was getting out of control now. The landlord of the 'digs' I was living at kept a high powered air rifle which he normally kept locked away. But that night I saw it carelessly leaning against a wall wrapped in a cloth cover. I decided to grab it and head off to the hotel. I didn't know what I was going to do. I didn't have any kind of plan. Walking through the streets late at night carrying a loaded rifle without a care in the world, I stormed into the *Crest hotel* foyer where Fred was now working as a night porter since selling his gym.

He tried talking me into handing over the rifle at which point, apparently, I pointed it at him. It was loaded and the safety catch was off. The result could have been devastating. I say 'apparently', because it was only recently I learned of this from Fred after I tracked him down twenty-three years later. My mind had blocked this episode out for over twenty years. But why on earth would I do this to a good friend? And to this day, I still have no recollection of doing it.

Fred told me that I was completely 'out of it' by then and had no idea what I was doing. Ironically, not long after that episode, a swarm of police officers entered the foyer but only because they were there for a party. Talk about getting away by the skin of my teeth!

That night Fred drove me to the psychiatric hospital in Bootham. He hammered on the main door of the hospital demanding someone help me. A male nurse came to the door who just kept telling him that I needed to make an appointment with my General Practitioner first.

This was ludicrous. How on earth are people in that state of mind expected to hold on for several days to see their doctor and then go on a waiting list for an appointment to see a specialist? By then you could be dead if you're suicidal. So with this, Fred decided to take the nurse to his car where he opened the boot and showed him the rifle. It must have had the desired effect because I was then admitted and led to one of the wards. They had just wanted to send me home. Several months before, I had slashed my wrists ten times and now I'd walked into a hotel lobby with a rifle. What more evidence did they need that I was in a very disturbed state of mind? Bootham was an old Victorian asylum with huge corridors and very similar to what *St Lukes* had been like. The driveway within the hospital grounds, bended and curved around leading to the doorway.

The bends were always placed in the entrance drives of Victorian mental hospitals to differentiate them from the stately homes of the gentry which usually had straight drives - hence the term, 'going round the bend'. I was in there for about four days spending most of my time thinking about Denise.

I sneaked out of the hospital grounds one evening and got a taxi to Denise's house several miles away. She had gone to her home although not as a wife. When I turned up on her doorstep it was as though they'd been expecting me. Her ex-husband was quite courteous considering, and asked me in. Denise came through and held my hands.

'Look at his eyes', she said. 'They're all puffed up.' I felt some relief after seeing her and was pleased there was no aggro. I then got a taxi back to the hospital and as I walked back on the ward, the charge nurse saw me from her office and said, 'Did you enjoy your trip, David'? They were hopeless with patients.

All we did was sit around all day being ignored. We were like domestic animals being farmed. We were all waiting for something but what? I was starting to realise that being an inpatient did more harm than good. The next day, I managed to find a phone book in the hospitals public phone booth where I got Denise's phone number and so I rang her. She was really happy to hear from me and this led to me recovering very quickly. Then soon after, she came to visit me which lifted my spirits so much. I was discharged from hospital not long after and soon we were living together again. It wasn't to last though and after a few weeks, she left me again.

One day I blew my top during a row and punched a hole in the bedroom door, leaving it hanging off its hinges. Denise walked out and didn't come back.

This became a pattern for Denise whenever we had a row. She would walk out, come back and then after several weeks, disappear again. But every time she came back, I was even more possessive because I kept expecting her to leave again. Then one afternoon I came home after a heavy afternoon drinking session to see her carrying her clothes and belongings to a removal van with her ex-husband in toe.

I noticed there was a police car sat outside which she had called knowing I would kick off. I went across to warn the officer to stay out of it which only fuelled the situation. I was emotionally wrecked and I started smashing things up in the bedroom.

A police officer appeared all of a sudden and managed to get me in a tight headlock that felt as though it was going to pull my head off. Shortly afterwards two detectives arrived on the scene and I was bundled into the back of a van and taken back to York Police cells.

Fred came down to rescue me yet again and made a deal with the police - that if he was to take me back to Middlesbrough, would they let me go?

They agreed and Fred had me back in Middlesbrough an hour later. I did feel a sense of relief being home, but I was hurting inside a lot. Still, it was nice being back in touch with old friends.

My coping mechanisms were non-existent. One thing I did have to cling on to though was a burning ambition to be a successful chef. And its ambition that has always got me through the hardest periods of my life. Work was able to focus my mind on something positive because while I was in York I started to train to be a chef. One good thing that had come from my relationship with Denise was her persuading me to take a job as a breakfast chef at the *Abbey Park Hotel* which became my transition from washer up to trainee chef.

I then worked at the Royal York Hotel and from then on my cheffing career took off. But I squandered every penny I ever earned; I partied every night and burned the candle at both ends as they say. I treated each job as a holiday and as though every day was my last. This would have long-term effects on my life I would never recover from.

Because I never looked after money or saved a penny I was never in a position to get a mortgage or be able to afford to rent a flat or house.

I had managed to go full circle with my life. I had started with nothing, had it and lost it all. I had been given a chance in life to make good and leave the past behind. But as always, I blew it. Now I was back where I started, on Teesside with no job. I was better off in the sense that I was now an experienced chef. But I had no goal or purpose in life. I was a drifter.

CHAPTER FIFTEEN

THE 'DEMON DRINK'

Whenever I used to have a problem, I would always turn to alcohol until eventually I became so dependant on it, I couldn't face anything without it. I would always use it as an escape from reality and sometimes as an excuse to cause trouble, with 'Dutch Courage'. Then I would blame others for making me do it. This is a classic trait amongst many persistent offenders.

Once I started 'going straight' and had turned my life around, I started to self-observe a lot more - particularly aspects of my behaviour, lifestyle and the role alcohol played in it. There were many downsides to my association with alcohol and pub life, but there were also many positives. Sometimes I would drink so much I would get into a fight or be asked to leave, or even be thrown out of a pub. But the pubs also provided me with an income while working as a chef. I just couldn't get the balance right.

I always liked a drink within social settings and I never drank in the house as this defeated the object for me. I never drank spirits either. I belonged to the culture labelled in the 1990s as 'lager louts'. I loved to pub crawl and visit various Inns and Taverns in different towns and villages which I was able to do a lot when I worked as a chef. When I decided to work in Edinburgh in 1992, I was on the verge of a serious drink problem and my bouts of depression were regular. Yet I somehow managed to keep getting work, although never for long. I worked at a quaint fifteenth-century pub called *Ye Olde Golf Tavern*.

157

Edinburgh was a fascinating place steeped in history as well as having a vibrant modern life with all the excitement I needed. It was also over run with football hooligan casuals from Hibs and Hearts.

Not being a football fan, I was uninterested in this, but I clearly remember them in the pubs I used to go in. I never had any trouble myself and it was only later I learned how huge this following was. This was also where I was introduced to late drinking hours which would be the worst thing I could do. I have never been anywhere that stayed open until the early hours; they even had a nightclub open until 6.00am. And some of the pubs opened at 6.00am in the morning too. For me, this was a real novelty.

I enjoyed working at the Tavern, but it was clear that alcohol was now becoming a major problem in my life. Some nights I only grabbed a few hours' sleep and hadn't had time to shower from the night before. I used to leave work hot and sticky from the kitchen and in need of a shower. But instead, I would go clubbing all night until the early hours. Then by the time I finally got home, I would be so exhausted from the twelve-hour shifts I'd worked and drinking binges, I just fell asleep. I'd then have to unlock the tavern early the next morning suffering from the night before to let the cleaners in.

It was while I was working here that the Scottish licensing laws extended day time drinking hours from 11:00am to 11:00pm. Therefore, effectively, in Edinburgh, it was possible to drink around the clock in the town centre.

I loved the Scottish way of life; the Scots seemed so much more laid back than the English. They had a great way of getting their work done and still always having time to party. They had a lovely warm attitude to life and one New Year; I had the best time ever celebrating Hogmanay. I'd never seen a New Year celebration like it. I had heard of the Scottish making a big thing about New Year and had seen the television shows at home, but this was something else.

But no sooner had I began to settle into one job, I would be looking for another. I worked daily split shifts between 10.00am and 2.00pm, then back at 6.00pm until we finished around 10.00pm. But rather than go back to an empty flat for those four hours in between, I went to the pub and stayed there. I often went back to work worse for wear trying to perform my duties in the kitchen, reeking of beer. Then at the end of the shift, I would help clean up and head off for a late drink at some bar, or night club just to start the whole process again the following day.

As with my uncle's journalist drinking culture, the catering industry had the very same reputation, particularly amongst chefs. Working in Scotland was perfect for me I felt, because of the extended opening hours. I'd never been to bars that stayed open until 2.00am before and night clubs that stayed open until 6.00am. Things got so bad, I once went straight to work from a night club to work a breakfast shift at 6.30am. Even the chef I worked with supped cans of beer while working the breakfast shift from 6:00am. I had regular money coming in, but every penny went on booze.

Pubs were full of characters, excitement and unpredictability, but alcohol controlled me. I drank every day and as often as possible. After working in too many jobs to remember during the 1990s and blowing all my money through my alcohol addiction, I went back to Middlesbrough for a while. Then one day, I received a call from a company called PGL who take kids' groups, providing activity courses and holidays. I'd applied for work as a chef when they rang me out of the blue one afternoon to offer me a job in Northern France. Of course I jumped at the chance. It was so laid back and great fun. I was living in an old hotel called *Le Pre Catalane* in Hardelot, a nineteenth-century hotel converted into dormitories for the school tours.

The people I worked with were all students on placements, or taking a year out of study to work with the kids. They used to teach them things like archery, horse riding, go-carting and take them on days out. They all went to Paris one day and I tagged along.

It was fantastic. I became quite proficient at speaking French because I mixed a lot with the locals whereas the others tended to mix with their English co-workers all the time. I felt that in order to enjoy another culture and learn about it, you had to become one of them. Then I made the same old fatal mistake. I met a local girl called Sandrine who was a young, sexy, twenty-three-year-old French girl working at a local restaurant where I used to go drinking.

She too was married as the others had been, but going through a separation. We hit it off straight away after she followed me one day in her car and invited me to go for a drink. It was passionate from the start where we would make love all day long - or if the coast was clear, we would spend nights of passion at her place.

The season was coming to a close, so soon we would have more time to spend together - or so I'd thought. I was in the same trap as I had been with Denise. As I have already said, I always attracted women who had marital and personal problems, who didn't really want to make a clean break from their past, yet enjoyed my company on the side. It was the same old story for years. Hardelot was seasonal and practically closed down in winter time and I became bored to tears. This was also a pattern that had developed over the years, an inability to deal with boredom. I was offered a chance to stay on through winter months as caretaker and I imagined a cosy winter with Sandrine in a country I loved.

Things didn't work out with Sandrine. She patched things up with her husband. She came to see me one day to end it and I never saw her again. The loneliness affected me badly.

I got depression so bad that it was one of the worst episodes ever. Whenever I'd had episodes before, I had friends and family around me. Now I was all alone in this huge Victorian hotel in the north of France without a single soul in sight. It had all the ambience and settings for a remake of *The Shining* and I was fast heading for another breakdown.

I remember there being hundreds of cases of wine in the kitchen which I set about drinking by the gallon. The season had well and truly ended, it was stormy outside - a complete contrast to the summer months only weeks before when it was bright and lively with staff and kids everywhere. Everything banged or rattled with the wind, and I was feeling unbelievably isolated. I had no company and I was getting spooked-out by the place. I kept thinking of all the history I'd learned about the place.

It was once occupied by the German army during the First World War and one of the previous owners had been killed there after falling down the stairs. At one point I rang the French Foreign Legion recruitment office in Lille. There was a poster on the office wall where I got the number from. It said that it took recruits up to forty-years-old, so I rang them and asked to join. I was told to call back and speak to 'Le Capitan' (captain) on Monday morning, but I didn't ring anymore. Then one day I chased an army *Land Rover* thinking it was the Legionnaires. I asked them to take me along with them when I managed to catch them up, but they weren't Legionnaires.

My mind was playing tricks and paranoia had set in now. Over the years I had always had problems with depression, but at some stage in my life, I had also started to develop paranoia too. I jumped at every single sound and after weeks of this and being in a drunken stupor, feeling hurt by Sandrine's departure and the isolation, I went rapidly downhill and cut myself up again. Self harming had become the way I dealt with pain.

I decided to admit myself to the psychiatric hospital in Boulogne which was difficult because of the language barrier. It was Christmas-time and I wanted to be back home with people I knew.

I remember feeling as though as I was in a deep black hole with no way out. This was one of my darkest moments throughout my history of depression. This time my medication was a tranquilliser in the form of a syringe. And I remember begging the nurse to inject me as I was feeling desperately sad. Three days later, I was taken back to the hotel but I knew I had to get back to England somehow.

Mixing with locals during the summer had paid off for me because when I needed help, one of them gave me the money for my ferry ticket back to England. Once I was back home, I was seen by my doctor who referred me to *St Luke's* psychiatric hospital again on New Year's Eve. After five days, I was back out with more anti-depressant tablets. Being back home helped me start to recover slowly and several months later, I found work again out of the area and got back to normal - whatever that was. I didn't think I knew anymore. What I needed to do was break the patterns of behaviour that I was stuck in. Being imprisoned can mean more than physical incarceration, you can be imprisoned inside yourself and repeated patterns of behaviour.

Over the years I worked as chef, I got to see lots of wonderful places such as York, Edinburgh, France, Corsica, Isle of Wight, the Lake District, and the Scottish Highlands where I made hundreds of friends and a girl in every port.

But I squandered every penny I ever earned; I partied every night and burned the candle at both ends as they say. I treated each job as a holiday and as though every day was my last. This would have long-term effects on my life I would never recover from.

Because I never looked after money or saved a single penny, I was never in a position to get a mortgage or be able to afford to rent a flat or house. I had managed to go full circle with my life. I had started with nothing, had it and lost it all. I had been given a chance in life to make good and leave the past behind. But as always I blew it. Now I was back where I started, on Teesside with no job. I was better off in the sense that I was now an experienced chef. But I had no goal or purpose in life. I was a drifter.

CHAPTER SIXTEEN

ARMED AND DANGEROUS

It was during the early 1990s while living back on Teesside, I noticed a new culture emerging that would start to shape our current problems in society. In grangetown and surrounding areas where I had spent most of my youth, things started to change for the worse as the birth of the ASBO culture emerged. It was a culture of anti-social families who were hell-bent on ruining other people's lives. And criminals were getting younger and younger. It was now 1993, and our area suddenly was no longer the peaceful, closely knit community anymore, but a place of fear.

Drugs were now rife everywhere and an anti-social culture was emerging with little or no respect for people or property and certainly no fear of any authority. Since moving into grangetown over fifteen years before, the area had now been ruined in just a matter of months.

Neighbours who had never needed to worry about being burgled now lived in constant fear. Law-abiding citizens now had to protect themselves and their property as burglaries and thefts were increasing. I needed to escape the area because I knew I would get into trouble if I didn't, so I was always looking for jobs in other areas.

I started carrying a loaded handgun and a knife around with me. One night I went to *Bennett's* night club in South Bank with the gun inside my jacket, carelessly doing little to hide it. Then, as I left the club, I was confronted by the police armed response unit who yelled at me to get on my knees with my hands against the wall felt something pointing in the back of my head while they removed my gun. I kept asking the officer who had 'grassed' on me and all he said was 'Think about David.' That was enough for me; I knew who had done it. I was then taken to South Bank police station where I was charged with being 'drunk and disorderly in charge of a loaded firearm' and bailed to appear in court at a later date. During my time on bail, I contacted an old friend I had worked with in France who lived in a nice part of the country called Wells which is in Somerset.

He invited me to go and stay with him to see if I could find work, which I did almost straight away. Also, this helped me when it was time to go to court in Middlesbrough.

I decided that as I got to know my work colleagues more, I confided in them about my forthcoming court appearance back home. I came clean with everything to my employers who were very understanding and gave me the day off to go and attend court. They even provided me with character references.

I believe it was because of this, I received a heavy fine rather than imprisonment. Being in a regular job with good character references to present to the court was usually the difference between being given a prison sentence or a fine. I was handed a fine after which I returned to Wells a very relieved person.

One day, my mother telephoned to tell me she had been burgled by some low-life who had kicked the door in while she and Donald were visiting York for the day. Donald had some of his wife's irreplaceable jewellery stolen too and I was now worried for their safety. Youths had started throwing stones at their windows, wrecking the fence and starting small fires around about, terrorising two elderly people. It wasn't just my mother's house that was targeted; others became victims of these low-lives. I rang the police on numerous occasions who did absolutely nothing. Myself and others in the area had called the police so many times yet no action was taken. One day I spoke to the police officer who covered our area about my concerns who said to me, 'Well they have windows too.' This was a first.

I had practically been given permission to commit a criminal act by a police officer. I'd decided to take on this new 'low-life' culture so I got hold of another gun which I carried with me everywhere.

I'd used it for committing robberies too but this had now become a thing of the past for me - it was old school. I didn't like doing this sort of thing either - but I was so desperate for money. I decided going after other criminals instead which was much more credible - the ones who ruthlessly mugged old ladies and burgled decent folk's houses.

So I tried to set up a protection racket and vigilante group. The drug culture was emerging fast and I wanted to start protecting the innocent. Too many good people were having their lives ruined by immoral arseholes.

Nobody was interested though. My associates were all settled, married men now - I approached the hardest and the most ruthless. But it seemed that the old school were fist fighters by nature - not shooters. I had always used knives in the past - now I was into guns - in fact both. I never much cared about the pain I inflicted on others. I was venting my own pain and suffering at the world.

CHAPTER SEVENTEEN

PARANOIA AND PERSECUTION

It was clear that this new 'yob-culture' was something even the police hadn't been prepared for and the laws didn't protect the innocent. Thankfully, my mother was able to convince the local council that they needed to move her to a nicer area, so they gave her a bungalow in Lingdale, East Cleveland. It was a lot smaller, but safer and the area seemed quite laid back. It had some beautiful scenery and I could see why some people would want to live in the countryside.

I was an angry person because of recent events, so I didn't fit in too well. I was aggressive looking and quite unapproachable and looking back, my whole demeanour was intimidating. I was of massive build, constantly frowned and didn't mind displaying hostile feelings towards people in general. At least this is what the locals told the police after my arrest - which I will come to.

But I had just come from a very hostile area where my mother and uncle, now in their seventies, were forced out of their home, terrified by 'yobs' and failed by an invisible police presence.

So now, I was always on my guard and suspicious of everyone. I was also very angry that I hadn't been able to protect my relatives more. I brought a lot of anger with me to East Cleveland and didn't even attempt to fit it.

It's a great shame because had I given the place half a chance, things may not have escalated as they did later. I was a different person then though. Even my own mother said I had evil eyes in those days. On the other hand, I was also immediately met with hostility and no-one really attempted to befriend me either. Nor did they ever get to know the real David. Because I had come from grangetown, I was called a 'townie' and shunned by the locals. This made me paranoid and bitter towards the locals and it added to my increasingly angry manner. Of course everything I am saying is how I felt at that time. My account of certain towns and villages and people are coming from the mind of a very different person to what I am today when I perceived things differently during one of the most disturbed periods of my life.

The *Lingdale Tavern* which was our local pub, had a reputation for great food, where people travelled to and from afar. But the bar always reminded me of one of those old taverns you see in horror movies when a stranger walks in, and the place falls silent. The nearest village to Lingdale was Boosbeck and I felt that this place was even worse. There were two pubs known as the 'bottom house' *Station Hotel* and the 'top house' *Boosbeck Hotel*. And if there was ever a place where I felt I learned first-hand about village mentality, it was here. I had worked and lived in small villages all over England and Scotland where small-mindedness was rife. But I felt at the time that this was the worst place of all.

Obviously I am generalising because not everyone was as bad as this. And today, I have good friends living in Boosbeck. But those who did show animosity towards me, used to all congregate in the *Station* every karaoke night. I didn't feel that nearby Guisborough was much better either, even though it was a bigger place. Apart from the very different accent, there was a clear disregard for outsiders from some of the locals. It was extremely 'clicky'. There were one or two pubs which encouraged this, and attracted the most bigoted. Small things would irritate me such as pub regulars always being served before someone who wasn't part of the 'click' for example. The cost of the grangetown new 'yobbish' culture had led me to a life of exclusion by a small group of small-minded people. But what got me really angry was the small minded few who treated my uncle as a crank.

Donald was one of the most educated people they would ever meet in their lifetimes. He certainly was in mine and I have mixed with some of the most educated people in the country. Yet they took some warped pleasure in ridiculing him behind his back. They didn't believe he had done all the things in his lifetime he said he had done. They couldn't comprehend that a person could do all those things.

These were people who had never left their tiny villages to try and expand their minds and it showed. Yet had they attempted to sit and listen to Donald who had travelled the world, gained several degrees and spoke seven languages, to name a few things, they may have actually learned something. I often wish we hadn't brought Donald to this area amongst certain bigoted folk who couldn't understand him. He suffered at being excluded and mocked and rapidly went downhill during his final years.

I did start to settle in time and so decided to enrol at *Prior Pursglove College* in Guisborough to study 'A' level psychology and GCSE French.

Here I was able to mix with a completely different culture. I didn't stick it out as I felt an access course would be more suitable. Access courses had become popular because they were designed for people who wanted to go on to university, who didn't hold the traditional 'A' levels. So I enrolled on an access course at *Redcar College* and though I worked hard towards it, I failed the exam. Realising that my life was again going nowhere, I once again slipped into depression. I started to drink more and more, but still kept looking for work out of the area. I managed to find work on the Scottish border for a short while, until another failed romance sent me into another depression.

I then found work in Gloucestershire for a while where I hoped I could 'snap-out-of-it' (a phrase people use who have no idea of what depression is). But I soon got fed up with the digs I was in and so I returned home. I started drinking more than ever and I was permanently anesthetised by alcohol.

Funny how things do continually come full circle for me though. Five years later, I returned to the area where I found a nice flat in Skelton, East Cleveland, not far from Lingdale and Boosbeck. And it would be one of the most settling times of my life. I enjoyed living there, I got on well with the local people and some of my fondest memories are of my time Skelton. I should also mention Kev Thompson who was a great neighbour and helped me readjust to normal living. The flats were all quite large and situated in a former school - hence the large rooms. But I only occupied one room where I had my bed, furniture and television.

When I first moved in, I had it all set out like my old dormitory in Wealstun prison. I felt at home this way - a sort of security from the past. Kev helped me by giving me bits of furniture; he helped me decorate and convinced me that I really needed to start using my other rooms - that I was no longer in prison. So instead of living my life in one room, I eventually used the whole flat. Kev and I became good friends and have never lost touch. But going back five years when I was living in Lingdale, things were very different. I was going through some difficult times. I had made friends with a couple in Boosbeck called Brian and his girlfriend Dawn. She had taken a shine to me and would make advances towards me when Brian wasn't looking. She would rub her leg against me under the table while sitting next to him. It was as though she wanted to live dangerously.

Naturally, I was flattered by the attention, but wasn't sure what to do. I was really uncomfortable about the whole thing. I even wondered if they had an open relationship because she was doing this right under his nose. One night she had fallen out with Brian and so approached me as a seemingly single person. We spent the night together, but it transpired that she had done this simply to repay him after their bust-up. I was a marked man now. I had cheated on a friend's girlfriend and as I wasn't local, I had offended the local community really and was now a complete outcast. The whole thing got out of hand to be honest and apart from the fact I should have avoided this situation, I handled it really badly. Things escalated until one night, I was in the pub toilets of the *Boosbeck Hotel* washing my hands.

When I turned around, Brian was stood there blocking the doorway. He had already threatened me that night when attempting to quiz me on what happened between me and Dawn. I wouldn't go into details and when he asked why, I told him, 'Because I don't want to hurt your feelings.'

Well the only way out of the toilets was through him, so I squared up to him to fight which he declined. At this point, the landlord who had sensed there was a problem, pushed the door open where I then came face to face with several others waiting outside ready to back Brian up.

What they intended to do to me, I will never know, but as they dispersed, Brian, said something to me like, 'I'll get you next time.' And it was that last remark that stuck in my head.

I had been prescribed *Seroxat* anti-depressants after my recent break up in Scotland where I'd briefly worked in Eyemouth, so I wasn't in the best frame of mind. I continued to drink heavily while on the medication, then one day, paranoid and angry, something inside of me just snapped. I remember feeling that there was no other way out of this situation, but to confront this using violence. I had never had such strong feelings of hopelessness before. In my mind, there just seemed to be no other way. I felt trapped in feelings that were so bizarre. I had never had such powerful feelings of despair. So, with bottled-up emotions and feelings of paranoia and persecution, I spent a whole day drinking around Guisborough telling everyone that I intended to sort Brian out and how I was going to do it. I remember going back home early that evening and sleeping it off. It wasn't enough though to shake off the dark, desperate feelings of no-return.

So that night, I decided to go and find Brian at the pub where I knew he would be. I also remember feeling an incredibly deep sadness that I wouldn't be seeing my mother and uncle for a while as I went and got two knives from the kitchen draw. I headed into the small village of Boosbeck and walked into Brian's local pub, *The Station Hotel* which was very busy, yet we both immediately made eye contact as soon I walked in.

I must have only drank one or two pints, but I was just topping up what I'd consumed earlier. I remember thinking of following him into the toilets and confronting him there. But at some point in the night, I decided to just approach him directly. I hadn't a care in the world about the consequences, or my actions.

Just before making the assault, I asked the landlady if she knew the number for the police. She sarcastically replied, 'Yeah, 999.' I responded by saying, 'Well you better ring it then.' She then got the shock of her life as I walked over to Brian. I shouted him pulling out both knives from my waist band then while thrusting one blade into his chest, I stuck the other in his liver and stomach.

He somehow managed to pick up a small table and throw it at me but it didn't hit me. Several of the regulars grabbed me trying to prise my fingers open from the vice-like grip I had on both knives while Brian lay on the floor behind me bleeding heavily. Years later, the landlady at the time told me she and some others had dragged him through the back and used tee-shirts and whatever they could to try and stop the bleeding. I hadn't a care in the world that night. As the other customers wrestled to get the knives from me, I eventually opened my hands to their relief, and they took the knives and put them behind the bar. I was resisting letting them have the knives incase one of them decided to use them on me. Not one of them tried to assault me in any way. But the thing that seems so bizarre to me now, is that straight after stabbing Brian, I went back to the bar and after handing over the knives, carried on drinking my pint of lager as though nothing had happened. I even asked someone for a cigarette which I lit up and slowly puffed away on.

And then engaged some of the customers in ordinary conversation. Something inside of me was relieved, yet very very disturbed. What had possessed me to do this? Why didn't I just stay away from these places and let the dust settle? Was I secretly provoking the situation? Or was I an innocent caught up in it all?

The police turned up at the wrong pub at first. They went to the *Station Hotel* in Loftus, but eventually did turn up wearing stab vests. They handcuffed me and led me from the pub. As I left with the cigarette dangling from the corner of mouth, I turned to the landlord who was watching from behind the bar and said, 'See you soon Martin.' Months later, when I got to read my depositions in prison, he remarked on this, saying, 'I thought it was a strange thing to do.'

And now years later, I have to agree. In fact as I write this, it's as though I'm writing about some else I have researched, because I can't to this day, comprehend who I was in those days. The landlady had told police that I was always staring at her but I suppose she thought she was so attractive and irresistible I couldn't resist. The truth was, I disliked her type and would often wonder what on earth a nice guy like Martin the landlord was doing with her. I actually felt sorry for him because he was a nice lad and didn't deserve any of this. Everyone interviewed by the police told them I was always staring at people. I had this habit in those days. I was constantly observing individuals and their behaviour. So their comments were true, but who cares? My curiosity for human behaviour led me on to become a social scientist and writer.

That night, while sat in the back of the police van, one of the officers standing outside called out to me, 'is this your usual forte Honeywell?' He then went back inside the pub to get some witness statements and I waited with the other officer with the van doors wide open, when I saw paramedics carrying a stretcher to the ambulance. I was then driven to South Bank Police station to face some heavy questioning the next day.

The police don't waste their time questioning someone who has had a skin-full of booze, so you basically sleep it off and go through everything with your solicitor the next day. Unlike previous arrests, this time all my clothes were removed and taken for forensic evidence. I was given some white disposable coveralls with slippers to match. My new attire was boiling, I was constantly sweating. It was a hot July day and bizarrely, exactly ten years to the day I was released from Durham Prison. They then took a swab from inside my mouth for saliva explaining that if I was found not guilty, it would be destroyed.

By the tone of questioning from CID, it was inevitable that I was going to get the book thrown at me and I was charged with attempted murder. They had tried to use the fact I'd told the landlady to call the police and not an ambulance as well, that I had intended to kill him. They were right too and I expected about ten years in prison for this. I showed no remorse at the time. Meanwhile, my mother had the police at her house in Lingdale searching for my antidepressants to bring to me. While I was sat in Guisborough cells, I could hear the officers nattering away. I remember thinking all the time how I wish I could have turned out like them and just lived a normal life with a good career. I never had an issue with the police, they had a job to do and that's all there was to it. The police were okay with me at Guisborough.

Feelings were running high locally, so I was flanked by several police officers in court the next day and not surprisingly, there was no application for bail. I was then remanded for three weeks and taken to Holme House prison.

CHAPTER EIGHTEEN

CHANGING PRISON CULTURE

HMP Holme House was a fairly new prison at the time. It had four house blocks, and housed both remand and convicted prisoners on separate blocks (as Durham did). The convicted block was nicknamed 'the dark side'. Two police officers took me to the reception entrance where I was to be processed. Inside there were other prisoners also waiting and I noticed to my left, a small room with a few prisoners inside who didn't seem to belong.

I later discovered they were sex offenders. The handcuffs which had cut deep into my wrists leaving a red groove around my wrists were unlocked and removed by one of the police officers as I was ceremoniously handed over to the Her Majesty's Prison Service. I noticed another much larger room, which was a holding cell, opposite the reception desk full of other prisoners waiting anxiously to get allocated to their cells that offered more comfort than being herded around like sheep in reception.

I was taken to the holding cell which had plastic windows, no ventilation and got quite cramped as it filled up. We were crammed in like a tin of sardines. One strange thing was that, I hadn't been there ten minutes when I started to recognise some familiar faces from twelve years earlier during my time in Durham and Low Newton. They also recognised me nodding in acknowledgment as though I had never left. All the echoing and banter was coming back to me like it was yesterday. Eventually, my name was called to go back to reception where all my personal belongings (property) were emptied on the desk in front of me from the large police polythene bag and listed. They then handed me property I was allowed to keep and confiscated what I couldn't keep. They took my finger prints again which I didn't understand because the police had already done that. Once they were finished, I was told I was allowed to still wear my own clothes because I was on remand.

It was clear to me that prison had changed in many ways, but in other ways, time had stood still. The staff and inmate culture had changed beyond recognition yet some of the same procedures had remained the same. The familiar prison slang was coming back to me. Prison has its own language that you get used to over time. It's a slang that was still the same, but with a few additional modern terms.

Prisoners still ranted on about how they'd be out in less than a few weeks and how they were all innocent, how they had been framed by the police, or grassed up by someone. A doctor, now and inmate, was sitting directly opposite me who had been charged for selling prescriptions to drug users. I noticed he was wearing a rather expensive gold wrist watch and I remember thinking that it wouldn't be on him for long. I also noticed a few of the prisoners had been allowed to keep electrical radios and tape recorders from their property. I was a bit baffled, because I thought prison would be exactly the same as when I left it all those years ago when we were only allowed battery operated radios.

Obviously, these lads knew the score and had made sure they had brought a radio with them. Before you're transferred to prison, you're family can take things you request to the police station which is all put into the polythene bags and taken with you in the police van to prison. Once you're in reception, they go through what is and isn't allowed to be kept in your cell. The rest is left in your property for when you're released. Some things are just confiscated altogether. For example, I had an aerosol of shaving foam which was confiscated because it could be used to spray at someone. The bags were then fastened tight with a security tag.

It was weird because I was experiencing similar emotions to prisoners who struggle to re-adjust to all the new changes in the outside world after serving a long stretch. In contrast, I was trying to re-adjust to all the changes that had taken place on the inside (prison) world, after a long stint outside. It also made me realise that if you ever upset someone in prison, it would never go away because someone would always recognise your face. We were allocated cell numbers and landings and of course our own personal identification numbers which is what we had now become, a number. I was no longer a person. I was taken straight to the hospital wing which was one scary place.

Because of my medical history with depression, as usual, and because of the seriousness of my offence, I was taken to the hospital wing to be assessed as to whether I was suicidal or a danger to others. I was then taken to see the doctor the next morning. I noticed he had a box of my antidepressants I'd been taking before being brought to prison, on his desk.

The police had arranged to collect them from my mother's home which they gave to the prison staff who then passed them on to the hospital staff. He picked the box up, took one look at it and threw them to one side, saying, 'You don't need those.' I later learned that there had been some research into *Seroxat* after people had complained of serious side-effects including, suicidal thoughts, aggression and increased depression. He may have actually been doing me a favour.

The hospital wing had some very odd characters and, as in 1983 when I was in Thorpe Arch's hospital wing, I was oblivious to who I was sharing with. I was in a cell with a young lad who suffered from epilepsy.

They deliberately put him in with me as they felt I was one of the most sensible inmates. And so they thought I could take care of him if he had an epileptic attack. I have no idea what he was in for, even to this day. They didn't really talk about things like that on the hospital wing, unlike the main population.

Bored and restless, I would wander around the corridors and chat to people. I later discovered that there was a paedophile ring on the wing, a former prison officer who had chopped his wife into pieces and someone who I'd recognised from the television who had torched his house burning his three kids to death.

One day, as I was walking along the corridor, a prisoner called out to me from the open food hatch of his cell door and asked me for a cigarette. I had noticed that he was always behind his door, but hadn't given it a second thought. I handed him a cigarette, at which point a male nurse hastily approached telling me not to go anywhere near him again. I could see in his eyes that he was trying to tell me something, but wasn't allowed to explain why he had made such a statement.

He said, 'He is a very nasty piece of work, stay well away from him.' I did as he said, and it turned out that he was a brutal rapist who had infected one of his cellmates after raping him too. Had anyone ever tried that with me, I would have killed them without giving it a single thought. Thankfully, I wasn't on there very long before I was transferred to the remand wing, House Block Two - A2 wing. I'd had an interview with a psychiatrist who felt I was fit to be sent across to the remand wing. I had made my mind up to continue my studies as I had been doing in college two years before.

I have a genuine fascination for human behaviour, and because I had been studying psychology at college, I continued working towards an 'A' level through the education department. I waded through Richard Gross's book, *Psychology: The Science of Mind and Behaviour* which I had been reading in the police cells. It gave me some interesting insight into people's behaviour which I could see in my fellow inmates, myself, prison officers and other staff.

I was surprised to see how lax things had become over the years. Remand prisoners were walking around wearing Bermuda shorts and flip-flops as though they were on holiday somewhere. I'm sure many would argue that prison is like a holiday camp anyway, but only those who have never served time in a prison say this. I think they were just exploiting their right to wear what they want while on remand. It was a hot summer too at the back end of July.

One thing I learned was that unfortunately, prison is just an occupational hazard to most criminals. You see them being brought on to the landing after being remanded by the courts full of pride that they've managed to get themselves locked up yet again, pleased to see their friends and familiar faces all eager to congratulate them for getting themselves another stint behind bars.

You hear them shouting and see them sticking their thumbs up to each other as the screw unlocks the landing gate for them to go and join the rest of their comrades. There's an old saying in prison, which goes, 'There's hard time and there's easy time,' and in my experience, there's some truth in this saying. The trouble is, your sentence can be made twice as difficult by some of the inmates who can't do their own time, yet are quite happy to keep going back inside.

There's also another saying, 'If you can't do the time, don't do the crime.' It also amazed me how prisoners adopted their own hierarchy of who should rank where within the prison culture league. They think this hierarchy justifies them to meter out punishment to prisoners lower down the scale.

For example, why burglars think its okay to target a fellow prisoner whose in for a crime they are repulsed by, I'll never know. All criminals have victims no matter what their offences are and it is not their place to judge. It's almost their way of justifying their own crimes.

When a burglar has broken into a family home, ransacked it, damaged property for fun and stolen family jewellery and irreplaceable keepsakes, how can they possibly have any say over how other inmates should be punished? No prisoner has the right to decide who should be punished, whether they have committed fraud, violence or burglary, no one has the right to set themselves above others.

I saw men scalded and beaten while on remand because of their 'alleged' offences, who later went on to be acquitted. One man was continually attacked by other prisoners because he was charged with rape. He repeatedly swore his innocence and took a personal stand against his attackers by refusing to go on the Rule 43, vulnerable prisoner (VP) wing. Rule 43 was the term for protection and those on it would be housed on a segregated block. Prisoners could request to go on it for their own safety if they wanted (now called Prison Rule 45). When his trial came up, his so-called rape victim admitted she'd lied so he was acquitted. Prisoners know better than anyone what false allegations can do to a person, yet they never give their fellow inmates the benefit of the doubt. And prisoners dish out worse punishments to what most the general public would ever seek to do. Another incident took place where someone was accused of hurting a baby at some point in his life.

One night I heard someone shouting accusations at him through the bars. Then the next day after we were leaving the exercise yard after our daily, hourly outdoors walk and intake of fresh air, I noticed a commotion in the passageway leading to the landing on the 'one's. I could see the young lad being kicked and punched by several others.

This blatant act of violence made me realise just how unpredictable attacks in prison could be nowadays. Apparently, one of the screws later checked the victim's records and informed the others that they had been mistaken. There was too much brainless behaviour in there. One night, a young lad decided to keep everyone awake all night by hammering on his cell door and screaming at the top of his voice.

People were shouting at him to shut-up, but this just fuelled him even more to hurl insults back. The next morning standing in the breakfast queue everyone was looking bleary eyed, when one of the older prisoners suddenly remembered the young lads taunts towards him the night before. With that, he suddenly walked across to him carrying his food tray and said, 'Yes I will by the way!'

At that point he slapped him across the face twice. I was expecting the screws to intervene. I looked at one of them who was standing close by, but he just laughed and turned a blind eye. I guess he was aware of his infantile prank. Sometimes it was easier for the screws to just turn a blind eye. But there were times when I wondered if the screws were any better than the inmates.

One evening during association time, there was some shouting and banging coming from the pool room of the opposite house block. That section of the landing was separated from ours. I saw someone get pushed out of the pool room door and fall to his knees after being struck with a pool cue. Then someone threw a pint mug of scalding water in another man's face.

The screws from our side of the landing quickly unlocked the gates to get across and deal with it. But the most alarming thing I thought was the fact there was no screw in sight over where the trouble had happened. This had escalated because apparently the scalded prisoner had been locked up for kidnapping his own children. But when the police chased him, he ran from his car leaving his children locked in the rear boot.

How accurate this was, who knows? But what I do know was, the screw who was supposedly overseeing the other house block, had deliberately wandered off somewhere knowing what was about to happen. A lot of people would be surprised that a prison officer would do this, but I have seen it first-hand. When I was at court waiting to be sentenced, one of the screws asked me if I would attack one of the other prisoners for him because he had swindled his mother-in-law out of some money. I didn't of course. I had more sense.

Most prisoners just want to get their heads down and do their time. You tend to find that the prisoners who are serving the longest sentences, in main, just get on with it. Most of the screws, do their job well, are quite easy to talk to and helpful. But as in most jobs, there's always 'bad apples'. I also felt that the Probation Service were sometimes quite naive too. While taking part in an 'offending behaviour' group discussion one day, we were told that there's always an alternative to offending, 'We always have a choice.'

I argued against this intensely, because there are many situations where someone has had to commit and offence to survive, or has had to defend their property. For example, I believe that if someone enters your home wearing a mask, it's justifiable to do whatever you feel necessary to save yourself and your family. What's the alternative? Try talking things through with them?

I came across a couple of screws who were old friends of mine from my younger days in grangetown. One was an old school pal and the other was someone I used train with at the gym when we were teenagers. I didn't try to hide the fact I knew them.

My attitude was that, if the others had a problem with it, then they should have a go, or leave me alone. I had no patience with petty squabbles or childish antics, which were going on all the time. Sometimes it was like being amongst a load of kids who had never grown up. But it was always the short-termers who disrupted the equilibrium of prison life. And it's these persistent offenders who are supported by the Rehabilitation of Offenders Act.

Because of their short sentences, however many they get, their convictions eventually become 'spent' (which means there is no need to disclose them anymore). Whereas, those who serve longer than thirty months imprisonment, never have their convictions 'spent'. And yet it's agreed even by the government, that the longer termers are the least likely to re-offend. I decided to study the environment I was in by writing notes. Word got around that I was a bit of an intellectual and one day, I was approached by the prison social worker who asked if I would like to be become a listener. The prison ran a service where prisoners were able to talk to other prisoners about their problems. It was like a counselling service, but we were only there to listen, not give out advice. I started to get the 'bug' for analysing and researching. I also took up long distance-learning gaining diplomas in psychology, criminology and psychology, child psychology and counselling theory through a private learning provider called the *National Home Study* College. Sadly, years later, I discovered that all the certificates I was so proud of, were worthless. And that the college was under investigation for issuing certificates that were not officially recognised.

It didn't faze me though when I found this out, because by then I had gained two genuine degrees. But it made me realise my vulnerability while in prison and how my genuine quest to turn things around through education, had been abused. There was my family paying for course materials from what we all thought was a legitimate company, which was in fact a scam.

So here we had a convicted criminal being scammed by a so-called legitimate businessman, who was as much a criminal as I was. Sometimes, even offenders can be victims of crimes.

Too many offenders lack empathy for their victims, because they are so convinced they are the victims themselves. They blame everyone else for their incarceration but themselves. Many blame their upbringing, society as a whole, their own victims, the police for locking them up and the prison staff for keeping them in prison. While I was serving my sentence, although I could see this selfish trait in others, I couldn't see it in myself, though it was most clearly there. It wouldn't be until years after my release that the 'penny dropped' and I would start to learn empathy towards those I had hurt in the past.

The prison grapevine was the first social network I had ever witnessed with all its Chinese whispers, hearsay and false rumours. It was the fastest form of communication I'd ever seen and it created all the same problems that today's social networks do. Something can happen on one block and they will know everything about it on the next block in no time. Considering most of the prison population is supposed to consist of poor communicators in the real world, they were superb communicators inside their own little world. They had their own form of language too that only they understood.

They tapped on pipes to make themselves heard, and passed things from one cell to another using small containers on the end of string. If they wanted to pass something to the cell next door, they swung it using enough string for the other person to catch it with their outstretched arms through the bars. This would have been impossible in Durham, because the windows were too high and you couldn't get your arm through the bars anyway. There was more distance between cells in Durham too. The best you could do is put crumbs on the outside window ledge to feed the pigeons.

The prison grapevine causes fights, rifts, paranoia and unnecessary stress. But as I explained earlier, it was the short termers serving six, twelve, and eighteen-month sentences running around popping pills and being a general nuisance to the rest of us who were the biggest threat. For they couldn't hack their time inside, even though they were serving short sentences in comparison to some of the others. They were usually the burglars, twockers (car thieves), and those in for minor drug crimes. The term 'twocker', comes from its official term TWOC, 'taken without owner's consent'. All day you would hear the same voices shouting, 'Have you got any temys?'

These were temegesic tablets, which are painkillers. I never touched any kind of drugs in prison and was once asked how I was able to do my sentence as a 'straight head'. In other words how can one possibly get through their sentence without taking drugs? This was one of the biggest changes I noticed during my second time in prison.

Many of the prisoners were incapable of doing their time *per se* and a lot couldn't do it without drugs. They couldn't see a single day through without some form of sedative. But one of the worst types of criminals I came across, were the white collar criminals. These were convicted solicitors, doctors, business men and other professional people who had all broken the law. Yet were deemed to be better suited to easier surroundings in open prisons, because of their social standing.

They hid behind the system and their own superiority. Not only did they regard themselves as superior to the rest of us, but so did the criminal justice system which protected them due their higher class status in the upper echelons of British society. This is a side of Britishness I find despicable beyond words. A lot of these individuals had elderly and vulnerable victims and in many cases, not just one, but hundreds. Had these people mugged an old lady, they'd be beaten within an inch of their lives in prison.

So why was it deemed more acceptable to scam the elderly from their life savings? It seems that physical injury is regarded as something far worse than mental and emotional injury, yet the latter can often have far greater consequences for victims. It's the same as why people sympathise with physical disability, yet shun mental disability. A broken mind is far worse than a broken arm.

Back in the early days in Durham, although the prison regime was stricter, and the building was grim, dirty and old, prisoners seemed more stable and stronger. The biggest change that was evident now, was the dominant drugs problem in prison.

In the early days, there was the occasional 'nicking' after a cell or body strip search revealed some hidden cannabis, or one of the night- watch screws had caught a whiff of weed wafting from underneath someone's cell door the night before and reported it. But now, more than ten years on, there was evidently a huge drugs problem which was also associated to other kinds of problems usually resulting in violence. Much harder drugs were now being used such as heroin and cocaine.

Syringes were also being smuggled in and some visitors were using their own children as a way to get drugs through on visits. Another culture shock was the changes I saw in the population, inmate sub-cultures and regime itself.

The British archetype prison officer had long gone. The screws no longer strutted around in their immaculate uniforms, gleaming boots and medal ribbons displayed on their tunics from their military years. The former military style prison officer archetype had been replaced by casually dressed, liberal thinking screws. Many of them had no military background like their predecessors.

At least in the old system, you knew where your boundaries were too, whereas now it seemed that a lot of prisoners had no respect either for themselves or their fellow inmates. And used violence even under the slightest provocation. The younger prisoners were also very different to the young prisoner culture I had once been part of. They no longer kept their heads down, fell in with the rules of the prison, or respected the more experienced 'old lag' inmates, we always respected. They rebelled against everything and lacked any amount of mental strength and maturity. The other major thing that had changed since I was last in prison was that there were now female prison officers working on the landings.

There was always one or two working in workshops in the past as I mentioned before. But never on actual landings locking and unlocking male inmates. There were undoubtedly a few who had real power-trip agendas. But always being a 'sucker' for a pretty face and soft-hearted where women were concerned, I liked them being around.

Perhaps this is why the new male screw archetype had been replaced by the more modern thinking screw. Or perhaps it was just a sign of the times and people had changed. Either that or the *Prison Service* had changed their recruitment criteria. What modern, independent woman would work alongside the old-school, army-barmy, male screws anyway? Female screws were referred to as 'screwesses', and addressed as 'Miss', whereas male screws were always addressed to as 'Boss' - except in the young prisoner institutions where you called screws 'Sir' - where you never let them hear you call them a screw either.

Just seeing your favourite lady officer unlocking you and working on the landing could brighten your day up. I can never say I ever had any issue with any female officer. Some were a breath of fresh air - for me anyway. They got verbally abused by some of the more foolish inmates. One of the ladies once told me that they would shout things like, 'Show us your cat'! This was all part of the new breed of prisoner with no respect or morals.

Female screws were sexually discriminated against on a daily basis. And although I can't say for sure, perhaps from both male prisoners and staff. The downside to this new initiative had its problems of course as always. Some love affairs happened as a result and though I personally knew of some who had affairs with teachers, I didn't know anyone personally who had an affair with one of our 'screwesses'.

The only personal experience I can relate to around this subject, was when I was released, I kept in touch with one of my teachers. Also while I was studying on the education department, one of the teachers was pulled aside and given a talking to for being too familiar with me. There's been several press reports on such occurrences.

Women had a different approach because of course women don't possess an ego as men do and a need to flex their muscles. I have found this with police women too. I was always able to converse with women much easier than men. But some men found them a threat to their male ego, especially those who had no respect for women. I have never liked the male ego and all that machoism.

Ethnicity had also become a part of the new culture and I can remember a French prisoner coming on the landing. He was abused and ridiculed as he desperately tried to fit in by acting the clown. But this just made him an even bigger target. I remember talking to him when he first came in. He seemed a normal looking young man with a thick head of curly black hair who just wanted to be accepted.

By the time the others had finished with him, he'd shaved his head with a *bic* razor. And his behaviour had changed so drastically he was eventually removed from the wing never to be seen by any of us again. Every

Ramadan, we were given warning to respect the Muslim inmates during this time of fasting and prayer. We were expected to be less noisy and more thoughtful. This was nothing difficult for me, but for some it was.

The wing was run by a North-East crime godfather of ethnic origin. Samuel was an imposing figure of massive build and about six feet- four. He was dark skinned, had a shaven head and very piercing eyes, but not menacing.

He was very charismatic with a lot of presence but never threw his weight around. The screws got on well with him. First thing every morning, he was unlocked before anyone else and last thing at night was locked up after everyone else. One of his mates ran a bath for him every evening after we'd all been locked up for the night. And when we all went to the gym in the morning, he would be there before any of us.

At lunch time, where we were all rationed to four slices of bread, he was handed a loaf. The first time I walked into his cell, I was surprised to see piles of clothes hanging on coat hangers that he wore for court appearances and visits. It was obvious the screws liked to keep him happy because he could keep a lid on things. In other words, if there were any problems or skirmishes on the wing, he could sort it out. It kind of reminded me of the sitcom 'Porridge' and its character, Harry Grout who was the prison Godfather.

I had only seen this sort of thing on television, but now it was reality. I made no attempt to befriend him but he seemed quite cheerful and witty. He was originally from Nigeria and had been made to fight in the Biafran war at a very young age. He had settled in Newcastle as a young man so he had Geordie accent. One day he approached me and introduced himself. He asked me if I was expecting a life sentence. I was surprised at this remark, so I asked why he'd said it. He told me it was because I went about my business the way lifers do. What he meant was, I acted sensibly, didn't act the clown and just got on with my time. This is simply known as 'getting your head down and doing your bird'. His observation of me was later proved correct too, because I ended up spending the rest of my sentence with lifers developing a bond and mutual respect with them.

This was brought about through my mutual interest in education and writing with many of them. But also because I could understand how a lot of them had ended up in their predicament. I could relate to how after bottling things up, they eventually boiled over. And how I had almost ended up being one of them. The more I got to know Samuel, the more I was fascinated by him. His fearsome reputation was projected by the hangers-on and the young people in awe of him. But he was much more than just a hard man.

He was a highly intellectual man who had lived a life full of tragic experiences. I remained in touch with him after I was released from prison and got to know his family quite well. Prison was full of characters and everyone had a story to tell. One of my fellow inmates, Jack had been remanded for an armed robbery. He had done twelve years in an American Penitentiary previously. He had the presence of a man you really didn't want to mess with. He had long hair and was covered in tattoos. He kept himself to himself and no-one bothered him. He wasn't very tall and not large built, but he had soul and he had the heart of a lion. Also, there was always a bit of rival tension between those from Sunderland and Newcastle. I later learned that this stemmed from a lifetime feud between the two cities and sometimes they would hurl insults at one another. Samuel finally got to go to trial and was given two and a half years. But he had spent two and a half years waiting around on remand. So for the time he'd already spent in prison, he walked free. He had spent the longest time on remand than any other prisoner in the UK. I later met up with him in Newcastle but didn't see him very often. The last I saw of him, he was at Leeds Crown Court on trial for attempted murder after shooting someone over a debt. He was handed a life sentence with a strange tariff of four years. I never did manage to work that one out.

AIDS had also become a problem in prison since I was last in. As I observed all the cultural changes around me, I thought back to a talk we were once given in Low Newton about a new epidemic attacking the UK called AIDS. And how we must be careful not to share our drinking mugs and eating utensils with other inmates.

Now more than ten years on, AIDs had become a current day problem in prisons. But there was a lot more knowledge about AIDs compared to when it was in its infancy back in the 1980s.

Other changes included the installation of plug sockets in our cells for radios whereas in the 80s, we could only use battery operated radios. And when our batteries used to run out, we would chew them as it made them last a bit longer - at least until pay day.

Light switches were now inside the cells so we could turn our own lights out whenever we pleased, as opposed to them being outside the cells when we used to be plunged into darkness at exactly 10:00pm each night. We had a toilet and wash basin in our cells instead of the old plastic chamber pots and bowls. Pay phones were now available for prisoners at the end of each landing, as opposed to the two letters a week we were once allowed to send and receive. Knife attacks had also become a common occurrence in prison and usually over debt. Also because of the new drugs culture that had entered our prisons, random drug tests had been introduced called MDT (Mandatory Drug Testing). This is where prisoners could be unexpectedly taken from their place of work one day or from their cells to give a urine sample.

Two screws would just turn up and escort you over to the medical officer, who would then give you a container for a sample. Two or three days later, you would get a small slip of paper under your door saying whether you had tested positive or negative.

MDTs always used to take place Monday to Fridays, so some of those who always used softer drugs, now turned to using harder drugs at weekends because the substance was out of their system by Monday morning. Softer drugs such as cannabis, stayed in their system for twenty-eight days thus increasing their risk of being tested positive. Taking the hard stuff meant that they could have a ball over the weekend and be clear by Monday morning. The MDTs converted a lot of former soft drug users to hard drugs which then created an even bigger problem.

You develop awareness in prison of who to associate with and who not to associate with. The nastier inmates were like vulchers. They would be hovering around just waiting for opportunities to 'tax' (demand goods from), a new vulnerable prisoner who was an obvious, easy target. In other words, bully him into handling over whatever they wanted from him. One day, someone came in for the first time and was 'taxed' for his watch and other belongings. It was rife, but the cowards who took part in this sort of activity, only chose the weakest inmates. Weakness is something you can never show in prison. One of my cellmates, Steve, was seen crying several times and his life was made hell after that. Because he had shown some weakness, he became a target for many months to come. The brutality changed him as it does many who experience it - prisoners and screws alike. Several months after I was sentenced, I saw Steve again. He had changed from the energetic and often, upbeat person, to one who was withdrawn, pale and oppressed.

Six months had passed and my trial day had now arrived. It was 15 December 1995 and I had decided to plead guilty so there was no need for a trial. I had been going back and forth to crown court for several months now when I entered my plea and where court reports were requested. So Judge Peter Fox decided that as I was pleading guilty anyway, a lesser charge of 'wounding with intent' (section 18) should be entered as opposed to attempted murder the Crown Prosecution Service (CPS) was trying to impose.

He set a trial date there and then. And now the day of sentencing had arrived. The usual process took place with the journey to court in a sweat box, the long hours in the cells beneath the courts and the odd cup of tea and a bacon butty.

I wanted to take every opportunity to save myself from a lengthy stretch, so one day. I took advice from a fellow prisoner who suggested I write a letter to the judge to offer my own mitigating circumstances, so I did. Using my best hand writing, I filled two sides of A4 paper explaining in depth, how I had allowed myself to get caught up into a bad situation. And how I had allowed my emotions to get the better of me. Also, how I intended to use my time in prison to educate myself as a way of opening doors to a better future. Just before sentence was passed, the usher passed my letter to the judge and as he respectfully read every word to himself, the courtroom fell silent. After reading it, he looked across to me and told me to stand up. He then said these words, most of which are verbatim. But because of it being so long ago, some are words 'to the effect' of his summing up.

> *'You have explained to me your actions today better than anyone else has been able to in this court. You said, you allowed your emotions to get the better of you and that is what you did. I commend you on your attempt to educate yourself while being on remand and with the sentence I hand out today, you can use that time to study. I sentence you to five years.'*

As my sentence was passed, I felt as though the judge's words were very sincere. I now set my sights on achieving great things in the world of academe. I later learned that the judge was about to give me a much longer sentence had it not been for that letter. And it was then I really learned the power of the written word.

I was taken back to Holme House after I had been sentenced but my personal clothes I had been allowed to wear while I was on remand was now exchanged for dark blue prison clothing which matched the mood of my new allocation on the 'dark side'. After the usual reception process, I was taken to 'C' wing and although only yards from where I had just spent the last six months, it was in total contrast. Now I understood why they called it the 'dark side' and why my fellow inmates used to say to me, 'Make the most of your time on remand, because it's totally different once you're convicted.'

How those words were now ringing in my ears. As I was escorted to my new landing, several of the others were hanging around outside their cell doors. I was immediately aware that they were weighing me up. As I walked along I became aware that my physique stood out to them as I was carrying two heavy bags and my neck and shoulder muscles were flexing. This was the language of jungle life.

A muscular physique can do two things. It can keep people away and it can attract those who want to prove their masculinity and challenge you. The gym is the best place for this because if the next man is lifting more than you, it can motivate you to work harder. This is healthy competitiveness, albeit motivated by the male ego. Some however, felt that they could challenge you in other ways through intimidation or picking fights.

I was lucky to have a good cell mate on the 'dark side', but I didn't like many of the others. I had made a few friends on 'A' remand wing and it was a place where every day was different. Everyone was eagerly waiting to be sentenced and it was their optimism of what they expected to get at court that drove them on. Some were bitterly disappointed when they got longer sentences than they had expected. But there was always someone going to court and the rest would all be waiting to hear what sentence they got, or if they were acquitted. The regular trips to court broke the monotony of the long days.

From the day you are remanded, there are several trips to court where you would enter your 'pleas and directions' to the court and dates would be set. It's a lengthy and laborious process. Monotony is the thing I found the hardest to deal with. The days were long and boring. Even a cell search would break this monotony. The screws that did cell searches were nicknamed, 'burglars' by the inmates. They would turn up with a Spaniel sniffer dog and go through every inch of your cell taking all you're bedding apart and rummaging through clothing and personal belongings.

I hated my new surroundings and was already wishing I was back on the remand wing. Some of the others had 'attitudes' and congregated in their own little groups. The television room was where they all used to hang out during association where they would inhale cannabis through a homemade 'bong'. This was a plastic bottle with a pipe pushed through a hole.

They would sit there inhaling as much as they could and behaving like infants. Their giggling and pathetic banter grinded on me. Christmas in Holme House was mind-numbing to say the least. There was an ugly looking tree at the end of the landing, festive tunes serenading from radios and an attempt by the kitchen staff to offer Christmas dinner of sorts. Because I'd just been sentenced, I was re-categorised to category 'C' then given two choices of where I wanted to be transferred to.

It was either stay at Holme House on 'the dark side', or go to Acklington in Northumberland. While going through this process in the screws office, the senior officer pointed out that because I was charged with 'attempted murder', I was a failure. My answer was, 'At least I'm not a screw.'

There was always one or two screws who tried to be funny by making snide remarks which only highlighted their stupidity and ignorance.

As I started my stretch, a great sense of relief came over me and the Judge's words were left ringing in my ears which had given me a massive lift of encouragement. I had made my writing into such a skill, that I was even able to reduce my own sentence with it. But as I said, I meant every word and was able to prove it one day. Once Christmas was out of the way, I was finally transferred to Acklington.

CHAPTER NINETEEN

DOING TIME WITH LIFERS

I had been told some horror stories about Acklington prison in Northumberland, so I tried to change my choice of being transferred there, but was refused. The move was scheduled for 3 January 1996. I was on 'D' unit to begin with, but staying there would have just added to the misery of being there in the first place.

All the young, and not so young, short-termers were running around annoying everyone because they just couldn't do their time. To them, prison life was just a game and an inconvenience. I immediately requested a moved to 'E' Unit which was the lifer unit but also had longer termers too. So because I was serving five years, there was no resistance from the staff. 'E' unit consisted of mainly life-sentence prisoners who I would spend the rest of my sentence mingling with because their approach to life and prison and their maturity, suited me.

Lifers needed to be very careful how they behaved, as they had so much to lose and were always being scrutinised by the authorities. But as my lifer friend Dave, quite rightly pointed out, they didn't just behave themselves because they had a lot to lose.

They did it because they had remorse for their actions and were not interested in 'rocking the boat'. And of course they had matured over their lengthy years of incarceration. Very few of them had a string of previous convictions, unlike most of the short-termers. In fact most of them had no previous convictions at all. As I became more acquainted with a lot of them, I learned that the majority of them had at some stage in their life 'flipped' It was usually a *crime passional*, (crime of passion), which had led to their life sentences. Most were in for killing their wives or partners. Their profiles were completely different to the majority of the other fixed-term prisoners. I suppose in many ways, I was able to relate to them more too because I had come so close to being in their exact same predicament.

They were always walking on eggshells though, because they could so easily be returned to closed conditions from open conditions or go back up a category for things anyone else would just lose some remission for. They didn't have a final release date like we did. They were on life licence of ninety-nine years, but had been given a tariff. Some lifers will stay in prison for the rest of their lives because of the nature of their crimes, although few prisoners receive a whole life tariff which is currently twenty-five out of a total of 5500 lifers. Most receive a set tariff, and the length of time they spend in prison depends on this and whether, at the end of this time, they pose a risk to the community.

A mandatory lifer is someone who has been convicted of murder. Life imprisonment is the only sentence a court can pass for this offence. A Home Office Minister sets the tariff, taking into account the views of the trial judge and the Lord Chief Justice. The prisoner will have the chance to comment on these views before the tariff is set, and can take legal or other advice about this. The Minister may set a higher or lower tariff than the judges recommend.

A discretionary lifer is someone who has been given a life sentence as the maximum penalty for another serious offence. In this case, the judge will set the tariff in court. Section 2 of the Crime (Sentences) Act 1997 requires courts to impose a life sentence for a second violent offence by someone aged 18 or over. This is treated as a discretionary life sentence. For a short termer, or someone on a long fixed sentence, they may lose remission for misbehaving, which can only last for the length of their sentence, but for a lifer, it was a different story. They could be kept in indefinitely, until the authorities decided to release them.

They were all aiming towards being transferred to an open prison which was an essential part of their resettlement and where they would be tested even further. This was where they would get a taste of the outside world with home leaves, weekend community visits and work placements in the community, all of which I will come to later.

While standing in the dinner queue one day, I saw a familiar face coming towards me. I remembered him immediately as a fellow YP who back in 1984, was sentenced to life after a burglary had gone wrong. And he'd killed the householder who attempted to confront his intruder. I recall his presence on our YP wing in Durham being somewhat of an interest to the other YPs.

I remember them all eagerly taking a sneaky peek through his spy- hole to get a glimpse of this new lifer prisoner on the landing. He'd gone through the system since starting at Durham back then and was now at the other end of his tariff as a category 'C' prisoner. He explained to me, that because he was under twenty-one at that time of his sentence, they couldn't give him life imprisonment until he was old enough, so they sentenced him to her Majesty's Pleasure instead.

I was lucky not to be one of the lifers after what I'd done. But I found that I was able to empathise with them much more than fixed-termers. Some, on the other hand, were to be avoided at all costs. One such lifer who had served fifteen years started hanging around me and coming into my cell every day until one day he got a bit uppity with me after I didn't join him to watch television. I saw this as a weird reaction and from then on I kept my distance. I later heard he raped someone. My gut instinct was right.

I have to say that several lifers tried to get through to me with advice while pointing out to me that the only difference between them and me was that my victim survived my attack. My offence had been the same as a lot of the lifers and I could have so easily been one of them. Some of them were still too traumatised to talk about their crimes, but the ones closest to me, opened up, so perhaps in some way, I was able to help them.

I knocked about mostly with Dave who was serving life for murder. He had murdered someone during a fight which had got out of hand. Yet he was the most placid person I had ever met in or out of prison in my life. He was also a brilliant guitarist and had once belonged to a successful band in the 1980s. So many of these lifers had killed in what had started as an ordinary fist fight but ended tragically.

One day, Dave was viciously attacked in prison by one of his so-called friends over something or nothing. I remember it well, because it was the day, we were all in shock to hear that a maniac had entered a school in Dunblane, Scotland and gunned down a class of sixteen children and their teacher. That was part of his excuse for beating on Dave, but then we all could've done that. As I've said, it doesn't take much for pent up emotions and frustrations to explode into a rage and it usually is over nothing. There were some foolish gangs on the unit unfortunately, who had to go about in threes and fours.

These were the ones who would try and queue jump at dinnertime, the only reason being, because they knew prisoners wanted an easy life and had a lot to lose. So rather than be 'nicked' for fighting, the rest of the queue let it go. They were rats who had no contribution to society whatsoever. We were handed menus every Monday where we would choose what we wanted for the week by ticking boxes next to a list of choices. We were also given a polythene bag containing teabags, sugar, powdered milk and also a loaf of bread. This was a treat, because it meant when the doors were banged shut at 8:30pm, we could make ourselves some supper. We were allowed flasks too, so each night just before 'bang up' we would fill our flasks so we had enough hot water for the night.

One day, I heard a commotion in one of the cells near mine where someone was being accused of stealing children's Christmas presents during a burglary he'd done. Whether it was true or not, I have no idea. But as I looked out of my cell, I could see into a nearby cell, an inmate threatening to batter someone with a chair leg. As it escalated, Paddy, (an Irish lifer) intervened and got battered for his trouble. These little skirmishes often took place, but it was unusual to see a lifer involved in a brawl.

His face was covered in blood, but he calmly went back to his cell and slammed the door behind him. It was easier to bang yourself up sometimes just to escape the jungle outside. But as always, people make assumptions and if you did fancy some quiet time to yourself behind your door, you'd always get someone banging on the door asking why you're locked up. In their minds, they were prying to see if you were locked up for your own protection while waiting to be transferred to Rule 43, VP unit. Another nice lad, was John, who was serving life for a murder he'd allegedly took the blame for as part of a 'bikers' pact. It may sound rather odd referring to a convicted killer as a 'nice lad'. But in prison, you adapt to your surroundings and learn to live with one another. You learn to blend in and look beyond each others' crimes. And as I have said before, no-one should set themselves above the next man. In John's case also, if the story about him was true, then he was completely innocent anyway.

Because all the lifers had to move to a category 'D' prison as part of their resettlement, a lot of my lifer mates caught up with me at Wealstun open prison where I was later transferred to. John was one of them, but his resettlement back into the outside world ended tragically when he was sadly diagnosed with terminal cancer after spending something like fifteen years in prison. As time went on, you would see a huge lump growing from his neck. It was a tragic sight to see.

During his time in prison, his wife died, and now he was eventually released to die. Directly, across the landing from me, was Billy who introduced me to my future wife which I will come to later. Billy was always a good laugh. Every day we would have a laugh about something. He went through a bad time though, when someone from outside tried to play mind games with him, by telling him he had slept with his wife.

So much of this taunting took place where men tormented one another. I can remember back in Durham, someone completely losing it after receiving a 'Dear John' letter from his wife. He had to be restrained by several of the screws while being carried from his cell to the punishment block.

Another character in Acklington was a lifer called Dennis Stafford who made headlines in a notorious North East killing in the 1960s, which inspired the film *Get*

Carter. Dennis and his co-accused, Michael Luvaglio, were convicted of murdering fruit machine cash collector Angus Sibbett whose bullet-filled body was found in his Jaguar car under Pesspool Bridge, South Hetton, County Durham, in January 1967.

Dennis worked in the governor's office as an admin worker. And I remember him telling me he was working on his book while in there. He was the only inmate who was allowed a computer in his cell, due to having arthritis in his hands he told me. However, one day, someone must have taken offence at the fact he had this privilege and smashed it up. The lifers in Acklington helped me a lot by showing me where I could end up if I didn't get a grip. One of them joked one day that I had a big 'L' learner sign on my back ready to follow in their footsteps. But the very thought of it was just chilling.

They saw me as someone who was heading the same way and needed to learn from their mistakes. Their calming influence rubbed off on me and quite a few were published authors and Open University graduates. Some were incredibly creative and I often used to wonder what could have become of them had these talents been channelled early in their lives. It was their influence that made me decide to start freelance writing for magazines which I did from my cell using an old typewriter Donald brought in for me.

At first, I would hand write my articles and then post them to my uncle who would type them and return the manuscript to me which I then posted to the magazine editor. Eventually it made more sense for me to learn to type, so my uncle brought one of his old typewriters to the prison. And though I spent a lot of time practicing, I found it difficult as it was so new to me. I then decided to join a class where the teacher gave me an electric typewriter to work on and some work books that taught typing exercise drills. I was also teaching myself Teeline shorthand from a book I'd brought in. Soon after my new found interest, I began submitting manuscripts to various magazines. They always respectively responded to me by letter whether they wanted to use an article or not. While I was in Acklington, I also enquired about studying through an Open University course. I enrolled on a Social Sciences foundation course which was similar to the university access course I had attempted two years earlier at college.

I had been working as a plumber's mate in Acklington for a short while, but this wasn't for me. I wanted to pursue my educational dream, so I later transferred to the education classes where I did social studies. Within the prison, there were a lot of different workshops and classes where you could learn new skills and trades such as furniture craft, plumbing, upholstery and so on. But during my time here, a new governor arrived and suddenly things started to become more punitive.

More fences were built, segregating the units from one another, workshops were stopped completely and some classes were axed altogether. Yet while all this was going on, the governor was getting a brand new shower built for his office *en suite* which I had helped work on when I was a plumber's mate. After spending seven months in Acklington, a previous application I had made to become category 'D' status meaning I would be eligible to be moved to an open prison, was accepted. I would next be transferred to Wealstun open prison near Wetherby.

CHAPTER TWENTY

A PRISON WITHOUT WALLS

W ealstun open prison had previously been used in World War II to produce ammunition for the army and RAF. Since then it had been Rudgate open prison, then later renamed Wealstun (open) prison. It was next door to what used to be Thorpe Arch remand centre where I had been in 1983 as a young prisoner. Since those days, Rudgate had amalgamated with Thorpe Arch to form HMP Wealstun (open) and (closed). This was an historic development for the Prison Service. And had the effect of creating a Category 'C' (closed) side and Category 'D' (open) side within one establishment. Wealstun's whole-establishment approach was aimed at progressive transfer of suitable prisoners from the closed-side to the open-side.

It was an exciting time being made a category 'D' prisoner and I couldn't get there fast enough. However due to the prison transport arrangements, I first had to spend three days back at Holme House prison, *en route*. They were a very long three days. We weren't allowed anything from our private property whatsoever. After all, it would have been too much trouble for them to open a bag and hand you something, so it was easier for them to put you in a bare cell which was a close second to solitary.

I passed the hours amusing myself reading and writing. I managed to get one of the cleaners who was always hanging around the landings chatting to prisoners through the doors, to fetch me some paper and a pen. You certainly learn to appreciate the simplest things in life when you're in these situations. A simple pen and piece of paper made my days much easier. Then I requested to see the prison chaplain who started bringing me books that had been written by former inmates who had turned their lives around.

A lot of biographies written by former prisoners describe how they changed their lives after finding religion. But I never got the bug for religion, although I do respect those who have found it to be a comfort and have managed to change their lives around through faith. A lot of the other prisoners would sarcastically mock them, seeing it as a hidden agenda to try and get parole, but many genuinely found comfort through religion.

Once arriving at Wealstun, we were processed through the closed-side first. At one point, things started to look as though they were going to go wrong when I was pulled to one side. My records showed I'd made a suicide attempt ten years before and that I had a history of depression. At first, my Cat 'D' status was in the balance and it looked for a moment as though I was going to be kept on the closed-side. But to my great relief, I was told that as long as I promised I wouldn't try anything like that again, I'd be alright. My heart was pounding, because I was on the verge of being kept on the closed-side of the prison.

A lot of the prisoners in the open side had come from the closed-side. Sometimes that was a threat to prisoners who were acting up, 'We'll take you over the closed-side if you don't keep your nose clean!' we'd be told. Open prisons are another experience completely. In open prisons, you've got mainly so-called white collar criminals. Years later when I became a student of criminology, I learned that some of these supposedly white collar criminals had more victims than some of the most violent ones. A health and safety negligence often resulted in many deaths, old people were often victims of their scams and fraud, yet they were rarely treated the same as everyone else. This elitism stood out a mile to me. Some of these inmates thought they were superior to the mainstream prisoners. There were more educated prisoners than I had seen before and more who had money to spend which they took pleasure in letting others know about.

Some of these inmates included several solicitors, doctors, a county court judge, a jockey, fraudsters, businessmen and former police officers. Whenever a police officer came in, they didn't generally stay long. They were always recognised by someone and 'shipped' out immediately. I remember this happening one day when a police officer was recognised in the dinner queue. Whispers were swiftly circulating that a 'traffic bobby' was amongst us and within minutes he was escorted away.

Like I said, they saw the police as their enemies for putting them in prison. Yet they were surrounded by individuals who had scammed and stolen from the elderly and innocent. There was actually one former police officer I befriended who was never recognised, probably because he had left the police a long time before. I never let on to anyone else that I knew he was a former police officer, because I knew it would put him in danger. Others also knew of his past career within our close knit circle of friends and they also kept it to themselves.

The open prison elitism was sickening at times, but it also went along with an easier regime which opened other opportunities. Prisoners regularly made 'hooch', a disgusting homemade brew. The process of making this awful beverage was organised with such precision, expertise and team-work. The kitchen orderlies would supply all the ingredients such as juice from canned fruit cocktail, yeast and leftover bread, which would all then be put into a plastic container (like an emptied detergent bottle) and left in a dark and cool place for up to two weeks. In our case, this was underneath the Chapel altar. I sampled it once and that was enough for me, but some drank it regularly.

There were also nightly 'fence drops' where prisoners would sneak out of their dormitories in the pitch black to meet someone from outside the prison who would then hurl contraband over the fence to them. Each night the screws would sneak around in the darkness trying to catch them. Sometimes you could hear them sprinting after someone or running through the dormitory corridors to try and cut them off as they scarpered everywhere. One night, one of my pad mates met his girlfriend at the fence, sneaked out, had sex with her, then sneaked back in undetected.

During the night, every hour or so, the screws would come round to check on us by shining their torches in our faces while we were trying to sleep. They had to do regular checks because it was so easy to abscond as many did. One night, I arranged to abscond with one of my fellow inmates but it never came off. We thought better of it in the end. We could wear our own clothes in Wealstun and some of the more affluent inmates made sure they wore only the best gear.

The nearest equivalent to this in the closed prisons was when inmates would pay someone with tailoring skills a phone card or tobacco to tailor their prison shirts, so they could look their best for visits.

I started going to Chapel a lot with Dave who I used to knock around with in Acklington and I would join in the activities. I don't know if I was trying to search for something, or just enjoying another social activity -

probably both. I even converted from being a Protestant to a Catholic with Dave as my witness. But I can say that I enjoyed the friends I found in the Chapel and I enjoyed the activities we took part in, such as the services and the regular meetings. I even did a few bible readings for the chaplain. And sometimes we would meet groups of college students who would come into the prison to talk to us or put on a play for us.

The Chapel orderly, Richard, was a fellow inmate and his job was to keep the Chapel clean and tidy and arrange services and meetings. He also used to hide contraband whiskey as well as his hooch under the priests altar. Things like this helped us through our sentences because we got a laugh out of it. It may sound a strange thing to say, but we did have a lot of laughs in prison. It's what gets you through the long, never ending days. Some of the screws hated to see us laughing. They preferred to see us suffering instead. There was a real mixture of staff, some who would encourage you to do well. And some who just did their jobs who were neither for nor against us. Then there were those who were even bitterer than some of the prisoners. I suppose prison can affect all who live and work there over time.

In 1996, we had a change of governor called Stacey Tasker, who was a young up-and-coming prison governor. She became immediately popular amongst the inmates. I think she ruffled a few feathers amongst some of the staff who were against any changes, a lot of who seemed to disappear over to the closed-side. Oddly enough, they were the same ones we had issues with too. Even one of the assistant governors was arrested one day. She'd upset a lot prisoners over the years, denying them privileges that would have helped them and their families. One prisoner had once requested a home visit to see his baby being born. This would have been so easy for her to sanction because we were all category 'D' lowest risk prisoners. But she refused, and then herself paraded her own newly born baby not long after around the prison.

They say 'what goes around, comes around' though, and later that year, she had been found to be fiddling expenses and was subsequently paid a visit by the police at the prison. Someone got hold of a newspaper cutting of the report and pinned it to the wall in the education block - much to the anger of the staff.

Stacey Tasker was a young, forward-thinking, energetic, genuinely caring governor. The prison changed dramatically overnight with new incentives for prisoners, more privileges, understanding, and opportunities. I started my Open University foundation course in January 1997 which if I passed, would get me into university when I was released. I was actually accepted on the OU course while I was in Acklington, but the term time for OU study hadn't started until I was in Wealstun. I also chose to go on to the prison education classes full-time. There was a price to pay for this though.

A lot of the inmates went out to work in the community, in schools or on sites, but because I had chosen education classes, I was unable to leave the grounds. This resulted in me being more restricted than most. In fact, apart from a few community visits that almost cost me my freedom, I never left the prison for the entire eighteen months I was in there. I had restricted my own freedom for the price of an education. But it was worth it, because in the end, it paid off. Wealstun didn't have cells; it had dormitories with four, sometimes five men sharing. We had our own keys to the doors and could come and go as we pleased - within reason. Outside, we could roam around freely and we didn't have to walk in circles in maximum groups of three like in the closed prisons. There was an element of trust. There was a painted white boundary line about 200 yards from the main gate. You could walk out of the prison if you wanted, but the consequences would be added time on your sentence in closed conditions once you were recaptured.

Three times a day, a deafening siren would screech through the air which was originally used for air raids in war time when it was an ammunition site. When this happened, everyone had to go immediately to their dorms, and then the screws would go around and count everyone. If anyone was missing, they conducted a search. And if they couldn't find them, police helicopters were called out. There were many prisoners I wished would abscond. Some would 'grass' others up by slipping notes in the letter box where we posted our letters and quite a lot were not fit to be in there.

It seemed bizarre to me that after spending most of my childhood years living on RAF bases that I ended up living back on them as converted prisons such as Acklington and Wealstun. My father was actually stationed at Acklington when he was in the RAF. He said it was a dump then too. Wealstun open was split into two units, north and south. I was on south unit sharing a dormitory with three others. It was a long way from the confinement of a cell I'd been used to. We had large windows with no bars. At the end of the corridor were two swing-doors leading to several pay phones.

Phone cards were £2 each which we could buy from the van that came around on certain days from a contracted firm. It was a long way from the former execution gallows of Durham which was used as a tuck shop. Phone cards were now the main currency in prison (barring drugs) as opposed to tobacco in the early days. There was a football field surrounded by a fence which I used to run around thirty times every day as part of my personal fitness routine.

I felt free and could lose myself for half -an-hour each day while I was running. I lost more weight during that time than ever. It was very therapeutic. I could also see the Leeds United Football training grounds and academy just outside. One of the team's former players from the 1960s, Willie Bell and his wife Mary, were helping the prison chaplaincy by visiting prisons to talk to inmates and according to the chaplaincy were very effective.

One day, a larger-than-life individual introduced himself to me in the corridor after I'd just come back from a run. He struck up a conversation with me saying he was keen to get the right people in his dormitory, because he didn't suffer fools which suited me, because neither did I. His name was Brian Cockerill who was in for driving offences and who later brought out his own book, *The Taxman*.

He was one of the best cellmates I ever had. And, aside from his fearsome reputation, he showed kindness and a genuine care for those he trusted around him. I trained with him a couple of times at the gym, but it was impossible to keep up. One day he asked me to hold the punch bag for him while he laid into it and after about four or five punches, I couldn't hold it any longer. It felt like someone was trying to punch a hole through me. He had phenomenal power.

We had nicknames for each other based on a comic strip in the British comic *Viz*, first appearing in the late 1980s. Brian was 'Big Vern' a parody of London mobsters such as the Kray twins. The Big Vern character is a heavily built, square-jawed man with very short hair, sunglasses, a heavy car coat and a grizzled look. My nickname was 'Psycho Derek' another character from the *Viz*. We used these names all the way through our time together.

One day I twisted my ankle in a hole on the field while out running and had to encounter the dreaded medical staff. The walk to the cookhouse each meal time was agony too. But Brian, 'Big Vern' carried my plate and cutlery for me, and kept stopping every few yards to wait for me to catch up.

We had some good 'crack' at times. I shared with lots of characters over my time in prison and Wealstun was one place where there were many. In one corner of my dormitory, was 'Porn King' who was inside for running an illicit sex shop in Leeds. Then there was Eddie who ran a high classed, escort agency in Newcastle and while he was serving his time, his wife took care of business.

Another Teesside lad sharing my dormitory was John Scarth who used to get to go out on home visits. I knew it used to be difficult for him and others like him who went on these visits, because coming back to prison after enjoying a short spell outside, was a 'wrench'.

John was the only ex-fellow prisoner that I continued to stay in touch with after I was released and fourteen years on, we were still reminiscing. Sadly John died recently, but I will always remember the many laughs we had about our memories of Wealstun. He idolised our mutual friend, Brian 'Taxman' Cockerill and loved to talk about our days in there. As I said, we had a lot of laughs. John was one of those prisoners who could do his time and somehow never had a bad word for, or upset anyone. He was one of the easiest going fellow prisoners I ever spent time with. But he wasn't just a fellow prisoner and a cellmate; he was also a good friend who will be sadly missed by many people. There was always something happening at Wealstun. One day we all had to stop work and queue for hours to get a TB jab after it was discovered that one of the foreign prisoners had brought tuberculosis into the prison. No one was allowed on or off the camp that day. One Christmas I was asked to help with an event the prison was holding for local under-privileged children. It was held in the visiting room. Three of the lads wore *Telly Tubby* outfits, the kitchen lads put together a nice spread and it was my job to write everyone's names on sticky labels.

When all the kids arrived at the prison, they lit up the place. Our governor and several officers were there too and I recall asking the governor if it was alright for me to write her Christian name, Stacey, on her sticky label, not wanting to show disrespect. But she was fine with everything and had become so involved in the whole happy atmosphere of it all, she was even sat on the floor opening Christmas presents with all the children. Everyone had a great time with games, they all got toys each and as they left for the night, we all handed them story books and a bag of sweets. It was times like this that really humbled me and connected us to people who had far worse lives than us.

My mate Billy, who had been with me in Acklington, was now back home and when I rang him one day, he told me he had a friend who wanted to meet me. She was called Tina and came from Germany originally. I thought it would be nice to have a pen pal and someone to visit me, so we started corresponding. Things moved very fast and before long she was making arrangements for our wedding. Why I went along with this, I'll never know. But in prison you do cling to whatever love you can find from outside, so you don't have to go home to nothing. When the other lads used to talk about their wives and girlfriends, and I'd see them on visits, I always wished I could have the same as them. And that's why I went along with it, but I just don't understand why I couldn't slow things down. Only six weeks after meeting, we were married. There was no engagement, flowers or getting down on one knee to propose. It was all arranged over a few phone calls and community visits where we would spend several hours outside the prison every other weekend.

My probation officer at the time was very concerned about my decision to get married and tried to warn me about the difficulties it could cause. She asked, 'Why is everything happening so fast?' She was also very apprehensive having seen similar cases like mine. I was determined to go through with it though. I liked the thought of having a wife and home to go out to.

For the wedding day, I made a special application to the wing governor to be allowed a special community visit pass. He was a nice man and deeply religious. One day he showed me an old school photograph he displayed in his office which was of him with his classmates, two of which were Bobby and Jackie Charlton. He sanctioned six hours which Mrs Tasker later extended to nine hours.

Community visits were always a worry though because if you didn't get back on time, you were classed as being absconded, then you could either lose privileges when you eventually returned, or be arrested if you were seriously late. The only time I saw this rule waived was when snow storms hit the UK causing some of the lads to be unavoidably late. On 16 November 1996, Tina and I were married at York Registry Office. My mother and Donald stayed over in York and my sister and brother-in-law came along while my two nieces were bridesmaids. Some of Tina's friends were witnesses. After the wedding, Tina and I went into York for a few drinks. Prisoners weren't supposed to drink alcohol on these community visits, but when I got back to the prison, they turned a blind eye under the circumstances. When I got back to the prison, I had to go through the closed-side and as the screw let me in he said, 'Show us your ring then.' I was very happy and felt for the first time in my life, I had what I'd always wanted.

Sadly, I was mistaken and as time went on, the visits got less and less and I became more and more paranoid and depressed. I couldn't hide my feelings and some of the others would wind me up and taunt me with remarks suggesting she was seeing someone else behind my back. This got to me in a big way and I took their comments to heart. It was big lesson for me. You should always keep your private life to yourself. Some of the lads were extremely vindictive and as I said before, when they saw any signs of weakness, they would prey on it and now it was my turn.

After a while, I was able to move to what they called the billets, which were two man rooms. My pad mate, Frank, was serving life for murder. But the room was dirty and had been badly neglected. So, while I was depressed about the state of the room I was living in as well as the state of my so-called marriage, I requested a move to another room sharing with Mike.

He was serving life for murder also. He later told me that the wing governor, Mr Smith, had warned him that I was depressed. But Mike was okay with this. He didn't let anything get him down. We had some laughs. He'd somehow managed to acquire a large colour television from the screws' office. Mike worked in the kitchen at a golf course in Leeds as part of his resettlement and each night he brought us a beef or pork sandwich with onions and gravy. One morning he woke me up to tell me that Princess Diana was dead. I couldn't believe what I was hearing. We sat and watched the television all day. We also watched the whole funeral service on the television and I could see Mike, fighting back tears as Elton John sang his classic rendition of *Goodbye England's Rose*.

It was unusual to see fellow prisoners display such emotion, because you became hardened to hiding your feelings in prison. But while I was going through my problems with Tina, I was less discreet at hiding my emotions.

My emotional state was now in tatters because Tina had stopped visiting and writing to me altogether, so as time went on, I deteriorated and started to become erratic. I even had one or two confrontations with some of my fellow prisoners.

Week after week, I would change into my prison clothing ready for my prison visits that never happened. We always had to wear prison clothing for visits, so we couldn't mingle with the visitors and walk out with them. The visitors' would turn up at the main gate and then be escorted along the long driveway leading to the visitors' centre. Visiting time was meant to be a family event, yet some would use visits to be more adventurous.

One of our former cellmates called Mark, who was at the end of an eight year stretch, had fathered a child while in prison. As bizarre as it sounds, I knew that some managed to have sex with their partners while serving their sentences. When I was in Acklington, you couldn't help but notice certain activity between couples going on around you in the visiting room. They were discreet, but you could see they were fornicating. You'd see women straddling their partners lap while using their shirt tails to hide their bodily parts. I wonder how many children have been conceived in a prison visitors room.

Of course in Wealstun, some prisoners got to go on regular 'home visits' where they could spend about five days every so often with their loved ones as part of their reintegration. And there was also the community visits at weekends, but it was peculiar how some were able to get away with having sex with their girlfriends and wives in closed prisons. They had no regard for older visitors and children who were in there.

Prisoners who were expecting a visit would all congregate just outside, trying to get a glimpse of their wives, girlfriends, parents, friends and kids so they could wave to them.

This is when you saw prisoners happy and smiling and eager to make that connection with loved ones. I stood with them for six months on the trot, week after week, religiously waiting and hoping Tina was amongst them. I continued sending her visiting orders, hoping she would just turn up one day, but she never did.

Then one Saturday, I was called to main gate as my name was down for a community visit. I knew I'd sent a community visiting order to Tina, but I didn't know if she was able to make it or not.

This immediately lifted my mood and a great sigh of relief came over me. I now understood that Tina had needed to arrange a lift to come and see me as she had done in the past, because she couldn't drive. I was searched and then asked to sign a form which we all did for community visits. These were to take with us in case we needed to prove who we were should we get stranded, or break down and needed to report to the police station. It was to prevent us breeching our curfew and becoming classed as absconded. Excited at the prospect of seeing Tina again after so long, I anxiously walked through the gate but couldn't see her anywhere. I wandered around the prison car park for a while, until it started to hit me that it had all been a terrible mistake.

My heart sank and it was the final straw which led to a complete emotional decline. I went back into the office where I received an apology from the screw who realised he'd made a mistake, which was little comfort. All I could think was, of all the times to make such a bad mistake, why did it have to be now?' And why did it have to be me when I was at my weakest?'

My family tried to help me through this period by meeting me the following weekend and taking me home for a community visit back to Teesside. But already broken and emotionally disturbed, I just spent the day drinking around my home town of Eston. It was a sort of trip down memory lane too. But while I was full of booze, I rang Tina and received a cold response. I knew Tina and I were finished. It was a bad idea to make contact with her. I then continued to get drunk. Once I returned to prison, I was upset and depressed.

I started crying in my room and Mike was concerned about me. Shortly after, I decided to head across to the closed-side and request to be segregated. One of the screws was someone I knew from the open side and as he let me through, I told him, 'F...k the parole, I don't want it.' I was charged with being drunk and disorderly. But while in solitary, I was able to really gather my thoughts and reflect.

I started to feel myself becoming strong again. There were no prisoners messing with my head and I started to see things clearly for the first time in months. Each day I was given an hour exercise in a small yard which was all enclosed, so you couldn't see any sky or scenery. Just outside my cell, there were a few pay phones where prisoners' calls were always recorded. All the prisons could record conversations, but it was done randomly, whereas, in segregation, they always recorded your conversations.

Unlike the 1980s, we could now have a mattress in our cells, all the time, but this rule had only changed during my stay in solitary this time around. During those three days, Europe changed the laws and I was told I no longer had to leave my mattress outside my cell door during day time hours. I had a cardboard chair and desk, several sheets of writing paper and a pen. As severe as this may sound, it was one of the best things that could have happened to me.

My thoughts became clearer than ever. It was then I decided I had to continue my studies and divorce Tina. And that positive decision was suddenly like having an enormous weight lifted from me. I had also by now applied to be considered for parole.

I had my university offer on condition I passed my exams and had secured a place at a hostel in North Shields should I be granted parole. The last thing I wanted to do now was mess it all up. I had started to panic now, because once I had started divorcing Tina, I had to quickly find somewhere else I could live should I be granted parole.

One of the main conditions of being granted parole in the first place was that you had a stable address to go to. Thankfully, my friend Dave introduced me to the staff at *Stonham Housing* that was involved in the aftercare of offenders who needed re-housing either in their own accommodation or in a hostel. Two of their staff members came to visit me in prison and were able to offer me a place at their hostel. The original plan was to move in with my new wife, but this had to be quickly changed.

But although this was a great relief to me, I was still worried that the parole board would see my behaviour as erratic after getting married to someone I hardly knew and then divorcing her in the space of one year, while in prison.

I fully expected all this to jeopardise my parole being granted and especially as my probation officer had expressed concerns about me deciding to marry someone I hardly knew in the first place. The day after I had been segregated, I was taken in front of the governor. A letter I had written in my own defence while in solitary was handed to her, as I had done with the judge at my trial. When I handed it to the screw, he said, 'What's this?' 'An essay?'

Mrs Tasker read out the charges, commended the officers for their work and then gave me five days in solitary confinement, a loss of seven days remission and told me to go back to the open-side. Stacey Tasker was a very fair governor. I knew she supported education as I had spoken to her before about university. She accepted my plea to be allowed to return to the open-side, even if it was only to sit my exams. And then return to the closed-side.

I told her I was sitting my Open University exam the following week, so she allowed me to go back and take it, which as I explained earlier, I later passed. She had compassion and she was one of many others who helped me on my journey. She didn't keep me on the closed-side either, I was allowed to continue the rest of my sentence on the open-side. I always felt that introducing pay phones into prison was a bad idea, as much as it was introducing boilers on the landings.

When prisoners can ring home, all kinds of emotions take over and can erupt. You're all of a sudden connected to your front living room, where you can hear all sorts of background noises, door bells going and voices and then the paranoia kicks in big style. You hear the sound of the television in the background and swear it's another man, or when you call, your partners out somewhere.

The next thing, your blood pressure starts to rise and your mind is now racing. Your paranoia goes through the roof and the next thing you know, you're accusing her of everything, from sleeping with the milkman to screwing your best mate. Women become as much prisoners as their husbands and boyfriends.

The queues to use the phones were endless and you could spend the whole of your association time waiting for your turn to come up. But what was really upsetting sometimes, was after spending almost two hours in the queue, there'd be no-one at the other end when you called.

This just added to the frustration and sometimes if you were unlucky, you might finally get to the phone just to discover you had been sold a faulty phone card and have wasted your whole evening standing in a queue for nothing. Also, if you were at the back of the queue, you often had your conversation cut short when you run over time. The phones were disconnected at 8:00pm whether you were in mid conversation or not.

A lot of men think because they are in prison, their wives and girlfriends have to live the same way. But it was these strong women that made their sentences go smoother. Although it's wrong to expect this from wives and girlfriends, I could understand these emotions. One of the lads telephoned his wife one day when a man answered telling him that he was now with his wife. He went and hanged himself. What a waste. If only in times of darkness, we could see what lies ahead as there's always someone else out there, somewhere.

There were times when you would hear men screaming down the phone, working themselves into frenzy, completely out of control and paranoid. I went through all these emotions and experiences, until I felt it was time to divorce Tina. Not just because of this, but also because she had been abusive towards my mother and uncle who went to stay with her once. She even locked them in her house once and accused them of interfering in our so-called relationship.

That was the last straw for me, so in October 1997, I rang a local solicitors in Leeds and started divorce proceedings. Once I'd made that mental decision to divorce Tina, I felt an amazing sense of relief. From that day on, I've always removed anything that has caused me stress, because I know what relief it can bring. During this period, I learned the importance of never bottling things up.

I started to open up now and would regularly walk across to see the prison probation officer to talk things through, which I found really helpful. On one occasion, while I was sat with him in his office, a call was put through from Tina who wanted to know if I'd been released from prison because someone had put a brick through one of her window. But of course, I had an air tight alibi. I was still in prison.

I started to wonder if I may start getting trouble from her from that moment with accusations. But clearly, it wasn't just my head that she messed with. In 1997, electronic tags were introduced and I remember one of the office orderlies excitedly telling us that hundreds had been delivered to the prison. There were a lot of wild rumours as to who would get them and be released early. Those who were in for violent offences had no chance, so I knew I wouldn't be tagged. When the time came to start the project, hundreds were released early into the community. Then not long after, it was revealed that they had released hundreds of prisoners that shouldn't have been set free. So they now had to go and round them all up again and bring them back to prison. That would have really messed my head up.

I was doing well with my Open University work, except, I had to word process my essays. This was new to me as I had never even switched on a computer, never mind word-processed on one. I needed to gain some basic computer skills before I did anything else with my OU work, so I went on a computer literacy and information technology (CLAIT) course where I learned how to work a PC and word process. I was getting good results and every two weeks, someone from the Open University would come and see me from Leeds to go through my assignments and discuss things with me. I also posted some UCAS forms to several universities including Teesside and Northumbria, applying for a place to study criminology on my release.

Then, I started receiving letters offering me a place on the course on condition I passed my exams. I sat my exams one sunny afternoon in the education block's kitchen with the education manager, Mr Woodrow invigilating me.

The kitchen which was normally used for teaching prisoners cooking skills was situated next to the visitors' room. It was visiting time and I could hear activity outside as visitors started to turn up. I had only a few days earlier returned from the punishment block after my 'drunk and disorderly' episode. But I felt good about the exam and my mind was clearer than it had been in a long time. I had worked really hard towards it and I was feeling confident. All the education staff had supported me all the way through my studies. Several weeks later and with the same excitement I felt when my parole form was slid under my cell door back in Durham in 1984, my exam results arrived telling me I'd passed. This now meant I could take up my place at Northumbria University to study a degree in criminology and my life had now started to change.

In early February, 1998, I was sitting in class typing something when Mrs Topping came in with a small grin on her face to tell me that Mr McKnight, the wing officer wanted to see me in his office. I knew this had to be my parole answer. They had been coming through lately, and he was the officer who would tell me the outcome. He must have been relieved himself that I'd got my answer because I'd been nagging him for months on end, asking if my answer had come through.

While you're waiting for your parole answer, you're constantly on tenter hooks. I went through the whole application process over several months which included a visit from the Home Office where I was interviewed by a parole board member held in the Chapel room. I had to produce a dossier, which included several references from the wing officer, education staff and probation. It also included what they called our 'black pen' which was basically our personal reasons why we felt we should get parole. This was a golden opportunity for me to use my writing skills yet again.

I sheepishly knocked and entered Mr McKnight's office where he told me to sit down. Whatever the answer was going to be, it would be a relief. As he read out my parole answer, I was elated to hear those words recommending that I was to be released on licence on 9 February 1998. I could've hugged him, I felt so happy. I rushed over to the education block to tell the teachers what I think they already knew to be honest, and asked if I could spend the rest of the afternoon telephoning family and organising things which they said would be okay.

CHAPTER TWENTY ONE

LIFE AFTER PRISON

As I said before, your release day is always an exciting one. I used to feel sorry for those who were met at the gate by the police and arrested, known as a 'gate arrest'. This is where the police had evidence to arrest you for something outstanding. But inmates were warned beforehand that this would happen.

In most cases they were bailed shortly afterwards. But it was just the thought of spending so long behind bars and with all the excitement of being freed, just to be re-arrested before you've had chance to leave the gates. Anyway, thankfully, it never happened to me. A week before I was released, my cellmate Mike was set free on parole after serving thirteen years of a life sentence.

The morning of his release, we were both sat on our beds waiting for the 8:30am siren which gave the all clear for everyone to go to work - or for those being released to make their way to the front gate. When it got to thirteen minutes before the siren, I said to Mike, 'Just think, you came in here with thirteen years to serve and now you only have thirteen minutes left.' It sort of puts into perspective how time stands still for no man.

It was nice being released with my mate from the education classes, Paget, who had got his parole answer just before me. During those agonising months while waiting for our parole answers, Paget and I spent most nights talking about nothing else and how much we really wanted it - if we thought we would get it - and what we would do if we didn't get it. Because I'd already had parole in the past, then been recalled as well as getting myself 'nicked' for being drunk and disorderly during this sentence - I really did not expect it again. I'd even been refused a transfer to Kirklevington resettlement prison in Yarm - I believe it was the drunk and disorderly reprimand I'd received at Wealstun that spoiled it. Who knows though? Kirklevington is renowned for its resettlement programme where all activity is based on sentence plan targets, which are reviewed regularly. Prisoners have the opportunity to prepare for release through skills training and full-time employment.

Whenever a prisoner wanted to be transferred to Kirklevington, two screws came along to Wealstun to interview the prisoner personally. I thought this was a nice touch, but I was shocked to be turned down. I felt it would have been ideal to be closer to home and continue my education in a suitable environment which encouraged that sort of thing. I had done everything to pave the way for a law abiding and fulfilled life outside. Had they accepted me - I may have had a much smoother passage getting to where I am now.

I had been offered a place at Teesside University as well as Northumbria. If I had told the parole board I wanted to return to my home town on licence, I may still have got parole, as it was clear I had done a lot to change my life while in prison. But you stand a better chance of getting it trying to make a fresh start elsewhere - away from all your risk factors.

If you go back to where you committed your offence, this is clearly a risk factor as are your former criminal contacts. For me, my risk factors were everywhere - they're called pubs. I needed to show I was making significant changes in my behaviour and thinking as well as just making academic headway. I had also made contact with my father again as I felt that if I could change, perhaps he could have changed too. I had learned that through the passage of time, a person can change if they really want to. And although there are still many who think, 'once a criminal - always a criminal', some of the most hardened villains have proven this view to be very short-sighted.

I will never know if my father ever regretted his actions when we were kids, or if he ever did change in any way. But we managed to leave the past alone for a while to focus on the present. We didn't see much of each other after my release day, but he had helped me a lot by being there to meet me at the gate that day. Ironically, it was the same prison gate I first entered back in 1983 when it was Thorp Arch remand centre. Now I was leaving that same gate - renamed Wealstun.

My father drove me all the way to North Shields Hostel where I was to live. I had an appointment to meet my probation officer - Mr Evans - at the hostel who went through all the conditions of my licence with me - where and how often I had to report to him. He didn't keep me long as he could see I was restless and anxious to make the most of my new freedom.

I was allocated a room in a shared house next door to the hostel which faced North Shields metro station. I dumped my gear in my room, and then went for a drink where I met up with my old cellmate, Mike. My father went back home to Middlesbrough after dropping me off and it had all been a bit surreal being free again. I had butterflies in my stomach and so much restlessness.

All I wanted to do was go on a pub crawl. In hindsight which is always a wonderful thing, it would have been a lot easier to move back home to Lingdale and stay with my family until I could find somewhere to live. But all I kept thinking, was whether I would have really been starting a new life by going back to the area I committed my offence. And would deciding to go back to the area where my victim lived have prevented me from getting parole?

I realised later this could have been catastrophic. I went to visit my mother and Donald one weekend and being me - decided to go around the pubs where I was now well-known for what I'd done. Unsurprisingly, all the locals were against me for the terrible deed I'd done.

But it was this close knit mentality that drove me to do what I did in the first place. One good friend that had remained loyal to me came across and told me the locals were asking, 'What's he doing out'?

Of course I always liked to test the boundaries and refused to stay away. I had the attitude, 'Why should I'?

One night, Brian who I had stabbed, was sat with a group of others in a pub in Guisborough. I was stood at the bar when a beer mat was flung at me. There were roughly eight people sat at the table. I walked across and confronted them. Not one person spoke.

As I've become older and wiser - I've developed an unshakable fearlessness. In many ways this is something I need to be wary of as it's the very thing that could land me in trouble again. But I believe being reformed is about managing oneself.

I feel that a person can never become - one hundred per cent changed. An alcoholic is never NOT an alcoholic, but they can change their lives and live without alcohol - as many do. But to think someone who has gone through a life of major upheavals, catastrophes, traumas and personality changes - can then become a completely different person, is somewhat naive in my opinion. I do know a person can change their lifestyle in such a way their focus can change. And of course there is the passage of time and maturity to take into consideration as well.

My opportunity to start changing was of course my place at Northumbria University which I had now secured and given as an example in my parole dossier as part of my resettlement plan.

It had been quite an ordeal planning all this from prison, such as where I could move to that was distanced away enough from the area I had committed my offence, before the parole board made their decision. And at the same time trying to convince them that although I had made a big mistake getting married in prison - I still intended making huge changes to my life. And it worked - and although reasons were never given, I believe that my university place had done the job.

Several weeks after moving to North Shields, the hostel staff found me a small flat situated in another part of the town. I soon went back to my old ways though over the following weeks, drinking too much - except this time - I became much worse than before. Prison had been conducive to study even with all the noise and hyper-activity and worries that go with prison life. Now I was back in the big wide world where pubs were tempting me again - except this time, I was living near Newcastle.

Newcastle was a new exciting city to me where I now had a string of new contacts I'd acquired from prison. Like a *Jekyll and Hyde* character, I began to live a double life which would eventually send me spiralling out of control into an abyss of my worst nightmares ever. Sometimes I would also have periods of reflection where I would start training at the gym again and go running. But then I would allow the demon drink to dominate me again and undo it all. Life after prison for many former inmates is anything but a walk in the park. They have their freedom back, but they also face a host of challenges as they assimilate back into society. The most widely known obstacles to resettlement are employment and housing discrimination. On top of these things, there's often a feeling of frustration associated with small, everyday tasks, like using a computer or riding public transportation which are all things that weren't an issue while in prison. I can't imagine what it must be like for someone who has spent years and years inside.

I had only been inside two-and-a-half years, yet it had made a significant impact on me. I felt as though everyone around me knew where I'd just come from and that they were all staring at me. It isn't just about the length of time you've spent in prison that makes it difficult to readjust - it's also down to your own personality and state of mind and how you deal with things. I remember getting confused at the North Shields metro station - feeling useless because I couldn't work out how to use the ticket machines.

I was still married of course and the hostel staff were shocked to learn of this when I asked them if I could stay with my wife one weekend. Once I was released, I decided to try and build bridges with Tina. I thought perhaps prison may have affected us both in ways that made us behave abnormally and erratic.

At least now I was back in the real world, I could find out who the real Tina was and how I really felt about her. I must have had some deep yearning to try and rescue something from my marriage. But this had been thwarted by her being extremely unpleasant to my mother and Donald while I was in Wealstun. So even if she had been the best person in the world to me, my family comes first. And though I had tried to work at it since then, I saw her for the person my mother had told me she was. This was a vindictive person who had more issues to address than I ever had. But what new prison marriage does survive?

I was one of those people who could never understand women who wanted prisoners as pen pals, or to marry them, yet this is what had happened to me. And now she was living only twelve miles away in Ashington, Northumberland.

I kept thinking back to all the days and nights I used to wish I could be free to start a new life with my new bride. But these feelings had since been knocked out of me by her deception and neurotic behaviour. I was trying to recapture something otherwise all those hardships we'd endured while waiting to be together would have been for nothing. After all, I had always wanted to be married and settled down.

I visited her a couple of times, but there was nothing there. Whatever we thought may have been between us while I was incarcerated, had long gone. Such is the false environment of prison - I had gone from being in love and desperate to start a new life as a married man with someone I thought I loved, to being a lonely, single individual. The whole experience had been full of inflated hopes and emotions - like teenagers go through when they fall in love for the first time.

But Tina belonged to the old life - yet another mistake to learn from I thought. I still had lots to look forward to though, I had five months to kill before enrolment week at university. I found work at the *Cleveland Park* nursing home in North Shields cooking for elderly residents to fill in time and earn some money. When my time finally arrived to go to university three years after being sent to prison, it was a huge culture shock because I now belonged to a very different institution. There were still a few basic obstacles though. I didn't know what the internet was, I was barely computer literate and I think probably the only student who was still handwriting essays. I had never emailed, heard of word or *Microsoft*. The computers we had used in the prison education department had been, *Acorn*, *Archimedes* computers which were outdated over ten years before.

I didn't settle for a long time after I was released and there was a few worrying moments where I almost blew it. But with the passage of time, good friends and family, I was able to finally settle, albeit a very long process. I had become trapped in a double existence. I was a student by day, but by night, I was mingling with gangsters, the seedy underworld, drinking myself into oblivion and destroying everything I had achieved. This was the worst two years of my entire life. I had now developed some serious mental health issues that would later lead to me to being diagnosed with having borderline personality disorder.

This was meant to be a fresh start, but instead, I was heading straight back to life of self-destruction as though being swept away before having chance to find my feet.

Once I left those prison gates, I went back down the slippery slope. Such was my confused thinking - during my first week of freedom, I felt so depressed that I wanted to go back to prison - back to the simplicity of my daily routine. Had I become institutionalised in just two-and-a-half years?

I went to the local police station in North Shields on two separate occasions asking them to revoke my parole licence. To my surprise, they kept refusing and one officer even told me that he had checked the computer and couldn't find me, saying that I wasn't on parole and that I was lying. It sounds a strange thing say but, prison had given me my first taste of stability in years. It had given me a new start through education and now I had slipped back in the same deep depression I had been in when I was arrested.

One night one of my former jail friends who I met in the *Stanley* pub in North Shields, asked if I wanted some of the drug powder, 'speed' sprinkling in my drink. And for the first time in my entire life, I tried it. That same night, I ended up on the psyche ward of *Newcastle General Hospital* being observed by psychiatric night staff. The effect it had on me was horrendous. I didn't like what was happening to me so I had gone to the nursing home I was working at to talk to the duty psychiatric nurse who then had me admitted.

You never really know what a substance can do to you until you've tried it which can then of course be too late. You get caught up in the party atmosphere and ignore potential consequences - but I had never been a drug user. Several weeks later, at the *Stanley*, one of the barmaids, who was also a university student, told me about student bank accounts that first year undergraduate students could open and how I could go about getting one. The next day, I eagerly went to *Midland Bank* with my university letter of acceptance and my student loan letter as proof. Not only was a current bank account immediately opened for me, I was given an instant £700 overdraft with a *Visa* card and cheque book.

I felt rich. It also made me realise how very different a person is viewed depending on their circumstances. One of the main barriers ex-offenders face - especially just out of prison - is being unable to open a bank account. I was straight out of prison, but because of my new student status, this was overlooked and I was accepted into a different sector of society. I was still the same person and very much proud to be working class but because of my new student status - I was catapulted to the student middle classes. It sent me on an immediate rollercoaster lifestyle. Once the student loans started coming through - along with my overdrafts and grants, I became deluded enough to think I was rich and continued to live that sort of lifestyle. Slowly heading for a disaster, I blindly went on partying at all hours, day and night.

I became involved with underworld figures I'd befriended in prison and lived a life of wine, women and song - burning the candles at both ends, like a sort of Kamikaze suicide pilot. I'd never had so much money and I certainly had no common sense.

I had several one-night-stands and brief encounters with prostitutes. One of my associates who was a racketeer where apart from murder, arms-dealing and drugs being his specialities - also ran a brothel. I saw a lot of life I'd never seen before. I had everything I had ever wanted, including my own flat, women, money and good prospects. But my lifestyle would end all this as I continued on my downward spiral.

One night I was chucked out of a late bar for insulting one of the doormen. I was completely legless. The next day I went looking for him tooled up with a large knife and a CS gas spray. He didn't turn up that day but next time I did see him he rushed across to shake my hand. He was all over me because one of the other doormen had told him who my criminal associates were.

Apart from these occasional skirmishes, I was using my blank cheque books to buy goods and sell-on to pub licensees and the general public - running up huge debt with the banks. I befriended a local man who lived with a prostitute who used to travel around the country with me selling goods and making a profit. Bouncing cheques, we would buy *Euros* from travel agents, booze from off-licences and clothing from stores to sell on. In the past I had always committed crimes of violence, whereas now, I was turning my attention to non-violent money making means. My new identity on the middle-class university ladder had even changed the types of crimes I was committing.

At one stage, I was bouncing cheques from five different bank accounts. I wore the best suits, jewellery and never stopped partying. This lasted for two years and it's a miracle that I was still able to pass my first two years at university. I was able to live a completely dysfunctional life yet still go to university and pass all my coursework and exams. As always, it eventually blows up in your face. Now a loose cannon, one day after an altercation - I head-butted someone in the street. It seemed I still had that violent streak after all. Well they say it never leaves you.

I was arrested and charged with common assault for which I later received a probation order. I was also eventually caught by the banks and given several County Court Judgments. I hadn't stolen the bank accounts; they were all in my name. I just went mad over-spending and accumulating huge debt. I did then try to leave this life behind as my increasing alcohol problem continued to drag me down and depression was deepening. I moved to Whitley Bay to a shared house near the sea which I managed to get through the help of *Stonham*. I found Whitely Bay to be very therapeutic and I started concentrating on my fitness again - running each day along the beach to the lighthouse.

I'd been given yet another chance. I got another job at *Risedale* nursing home just round the corner from where I lived. And shortly afterwards, I started dating one of the carers I worked with called Janet. One day she asked me if I wanted to go for drink and that sparked off a romance which, as always, was complicated and doomed to failure.

Had I had the ability to think of consequences - I could have avoided so much heartache and trouble. Janet still lived with her divorced husband which I was always suspicious about and it didn't help my already weak state of mind. I was never sure if she was divorced as she claimed. But I could believe it I suppose, because her whole family life was one weird set up. I settled in Whitley Bay more and started living more like a student.

I would get the Metro train to my classes at Northumbria each day and I even excelled in my studies - at one point achieving eighty-five per cent for an assignment. During this time, I had become involved in a campaign to get Reg Kray released from prison after he'd reached the thirty year mark. This was all organised by his wife Roberta. Reg was at that time in Wayland prison in Norfolk. And as Roberta worked tirelessly on her part of the campaign, I did my part in the North East gathering hundreds of signatures which were later submitted to the Home Office by his solicitor.

The *Newcastle Chronicle* ran an article about my part in the campaign which I sent to Reg. He wrote back to me inviting me to visit him in Norfolk. I also spoke to a reporter from the *Newcastle Journal* to promote the campaign - but he was more interested in my story which really threw me. I couldn't understand why he would be more interested in me than Reg Kray.

Visiting Reg became complicated because his own visiting order was used up. He used to ask other prisoners to send out their visiting orders so more people could visit him. The visitors would then turn up to see Reg while the other poor guy who the visiting order belonged to, was left on his own. And it also meant his visiting order was used up for when he wanted his family or friends to visit.

There used to be a large circle of chairs gathered around Reg's table which was eventually stopped after complaints were made. The visit didn't come off in the end, firstly, because he couldn't get a prisoner to agree to this for me. And to be honest, Norfolk was a long hike from Whitley Bay by coach. I kept in touch with Roberta by telephone and sometimes our conversations were cut short when Reg was trying to get through. One day in 1998, Roberta got me into a book-signing event as a special guest to meet one of her husband's old associates - 'Mad' Frankie Fraser. She passed on a letter I'd written to Frankie who replied, telling me he was coming through to Newcastle and inviting me to go and see him. I continued to write to Reg until his death in 2000.

CHAPTER TWENTY TWO

BORDERLINE SANITY

My probation officer at North Shields had seen the signs that something was clearly wrong with me and was genuinely concerned for mine and the public's safety. I had a serious alcohol problem and I was in and out of court. She had me referred to one of the top psychiatrists in the country - Dr Kim Fraser.

He was a softly spoken man from Edinburgh and was based at *St Nicholas hospital* in Newcastle. I was intrigued by the fact he was once Ronnie Kray's doctor too. My probation officer had wanted him to give a diagnosis on me. The diagnosis was depression and borderline personality disorder caused by bad parenting, alcohol abuse, continual rejections and broken relationships. I was prescribed *Stelazine* tranquillisers which were used for schizophrenia and anxiety.

Personality disorders involve long term, problematic behaviours that typically are first exhibited during adolescence and cause marked distress and impairment. The very definition of personality disorders as 'chronic maladaptive patterns of behaviour' implies that symptoms are stable over time, however, recent studies indicate that symptoms improve and may even completely remit over the years.

Realistically, the last thing I needed at that time was a relationship - let alone a complicated one - with my sort of mental instability. But in my mind, I felt a steady relationship was the only thing that would make my life complete. One night, Janet and I arranged to spend the weekend together. I was 'suited and booted' reeking of aftershave and eagerly waiting for her. But she didn't turn up. Without a single word, she just didn't bother to contact me and I couldn't get in touch with her either. I was desperately sad and confused - sitting around in my attic room all day waiting for her to turn up or at least call. I was continually trying to contact her on her mobile phone.

When I was in my most vulnerable state of mind, this is all it would take to send me into a dark place. Two days later, she made contact and explained she'd gone to see an old boyfriend. This of course made me even worse. Had it been a girlfriend - I could l have accepted it. But an old boyfriend? Then to really pour salt on the wound she told me he'd asked her why she was associating with the likes of me? Of course - this was man who had cheated with Janet while his wife was ill in hospital.

Why is it those who have committed some of the worse sins are the quickest to discredit everyone else?

Had I managed to get the opportunity - I would have most certainly told his wife what she deserved to know. One thing in life I learned was - before you cast assertions at others - always remember that they may know a little more about you than you realise.

I have done many bad things in my life but cheating on a partner is not one of them. One of the most special things to me is a relationship, And though men do tend to think with their penises all the time - some of us do still cherish the love a good woman above all.

But Janet didn't cherish the love of a good man and these types of shifty things continued to happen where she would turn up out of the blue and then disappear for days without a bye or leave.

The signs were clearly there from day one - I just refused to see them as I had with all my other fake romances. One weekend, we went to visit my mother and

Donald which was an enjoyable outing. It was great to see them after so long. We were all laughing and enjoying ourselves when I decided to get the camera to capture the special moment.

As I went to take a photograph of her, she covered up her face and strongly objected which I thought was very strange. After that I started to become more suspicious of her - especially after my mother commented on how odd it was. For months and months, she kept me a secret from most of her family apart from her daughter. I knew something was wrong. I just needed to face up to it. The whole family arrangement, her secret meetings with me, her reaction to being photographed and not wanting to be seen with me in public, was all too sneaky and 'cloak and dagger'.

I couldn't visit her house because of her odd arrangements with her ex-husband and it was awkward telephoning too. She was supposedly divorced, yet still lived with her ex-husband, daughter and two sons. I was banned from going anywhere near the house, but if she was divorced - why did that matter? Was I so desperate to find a partner, that I would put with anything rather than be alone? It seemed so - even if it did mean being hurt and making a fool of myself which I always knew would happen.

I used to envy other couples who looked so close and within their own little bubble. All I wanted was her to come home with me some nights - or to be on the other end of the telephone so I could speak to her and to go out with some evenings. At least then I could fool myself into thinking that I was involved in a real relationship. This was impossible because after all - I was just being used. But rather than be alone, I stuck it out as long as I could, trying to cope with the abnormal circumstances. It was only a matter of time before I reached breaking point and when I did - I exploded like a bomb and got arrested.

I had been drinking more heavily than usual on top of the tranquillisers I was taking. I was feeling worse than I had in a long time. Then all of a sudden, I didn't hear from Janet for two weeks. I was now reaching that breaking point, so one weekend; I decided to turn up at her house unannounced.

I didn't go there to cause trouble; I was just missing her so much. She was surprised to see me, but not happy. And obviously didn't realise that I'd had the nerve to do this. It was obvious I was not welcome and after exchanging a few words, she shut the door in my face. I was really hurt by her icy cold reaction towards me and at that moment, all the months of deceit, humiliation and being made to feel small that had built up inside me, boiled over.

I noticed a large rock nearby, so I picked it up and hurled it through her living room window. I was now past caring - a feeling I would get whenever I was pushed too far. I was scared of myself whenever I got to this stage. Being scared of yourself is something that I can't explain, but knowing deep down that you could be capable of massive violence is a terrifying thought.

Things escalated as her family interfered, and then eight police officers in two vans and a police car turned up from Forest Hall police station. I fought with them resisting arrest. One of the officers sprayed me in the face with CS gas while others wacked me across the knees with batons.

The wind had carried the gas over to two of their colleagues who were now coughing and choking by a wall. The next baton strike brought me to my knees at which point one of Janet's sons ran over and kicked me - not while I was standing of course. I was quickly handcuffed and dragged over to a waiting police car. I continued to struggle with the officers, then I felt a hand over my mouth at which point I sank my teeth into it. I heard him scream, 'He's bitten me'!

I was then dragged into the back of the van where I was hurled on to the floor. Then came a volley of kicks and punches from several officers. One even stamped on my face leaving a boot print which I noticed the next day. I was taken to Whitley Bay Police cells where I was charged with criminal damage and assaulting a police officer. From my cell, I heard one of the officers saying, 'He's done this before' as he looked up my details on the computer.

I banged on the cell door for what seemed like hours. Then I heard the clanking of keys. I was let out and led to the telephone to speak to the officer I'd bitten. He'd telephoned the station from the hospital to ask if I had AIDS.

After putting his mind at rest, I was bailed when I went straight out on the booze looking like the Elephant man. Several weeks later my case came up at North Shields Magistrates Court where it was dealt with as a sort of mini trial. Just before the case started while I was outside in the waiting area, I went to the gent's toilet and who should walk in? But the officer I'd bitten. We just said, hello to each other and went about our business.

The police defence was a female solicitor who looked as though she had just left school. I got my turn in the dock where I was claiming that the police had handcuffed me behind my back while she was arguing they had in fact handcuffed me at the front. I didn't care if I was being sent back to prison, I just argued with her, but wasn't actually sure what difference it made how they'd cuffed me. I'd had photographs taken of the injuries to my face which included burns from the gas and the outline of the boot print. Surely this was more important than whether my hands were at the front or back when they handcuffed me? To no surprise at all, the police were not charged for assaulting me, but I was given a fine and a probation order. Twelve years before, I had my parole revoked just for something I said to my probation officer. Now I was on parole with two probation orders and a fine simultaneously. It seemed that no matter what I did, the authorities would never revoke my parole. This was a sure sign that times had changed.

The most curious thing about the trial though, was the reaction of two of the police officers when the court read out a quote from my statement. I had mentioned that Janet was divorced but as this was read out - the two officers looked at one another with a puzzled expression. The penny finally dropped. All what I had just endured over the last several months suddenly made sense. There was an officer with a bandaged hand where I'd bitten him, two of their colleagues with gas spray burns and myself - also with spray burns, a swollen face and about to get a hefty fine.

And all because of a lying woman who didn't even have to appear in court. But she would be seen as the innocent victim whose life was so badly affected by a convicted, violent thug. Her innocent looking, softly spoken demeanour would have fooled the police when they went to get her statement.

Yes I did cause criminal damage and assault a police officer. But she had committed perjury and didn't even have to attend court. Not only did I feel like a fool, but why oh why, did I put myself through all of this? The signs had always been there, I just refused to see them, and all because I couldn't bare being alone. Apart from the facial injuries I'd sustained from the police beating and CS gas spray, my eyes were puffed out with the medication I'd been taking. I was doped, depressed and mentally and physically exhausted. I stopped working at the nursing home as I obviously couldn't work with Janet being there. I decided to start knuckling down to my studies at that point. I had now reached the end of the line and needed to either carry on with my studies - or withdraw from university altogether.

After that Easter break, I hobbled in to the university to see my lecturer, Peter Francis, who since then has become a Professor at Northumbria. I looked like I'd gone two rounds with Mike Tyson. 'What happened?' he said. 'The police did it' I replied. His reaction told me, he wasn't that surprised. Then I asked for some time off to gather my thoughts. He agreed and I left.

Over this period, I spent all day, every day drinking myself into a stupor. I kept telephoning Dr Fraser's office at *St Nicholas hospital* begging for help. But his secretary kept telling me that he wasn't there so I just kept leaving messages - requesting to be admitted into hospital. I had always done this in the past whenever I felt in desperate need of help. I just felt that things couldn't be turned around.

Each time I telephoned, I couldn't get hold of him. Then two weeks later at one of our meetings, once I started to regain my composure - he admitted that he'd deliberately avoided my calls. And that he was in fact there all along in the background while I was ringing his office. He'd forced me to deal with my feelings of despair on my own by refusing to come to the telephone. He told me that I had an inner strength that I had never called on before because it was always too easy for me to get prescribed medication and a few days in a psychiatric hospital. I have to say, that ever since then, although I have had other problems in my life where I have grieved, lost and loved - I have never taken medication again or been in hospital or even seen a psychiatrist. I'm not suggesting that I was cured, but I had certainly learned to take control of myself better. And as long as I avoided certain relationships and I kept the alcohol to a minimum, I could live a happy life.

Dr Fraser's foresight helped me more than any other counsellor or doctor ever had. I had seen many others in the past who were never able to diagnose me. Some just said I was immature. I don't doubt that for one moment, but there was a little more to my behaviour than that.

Dr Fraser showed me that we just have to have a little more faith in ourselves and keep our dignity. I didn't suddenly have an overnight miracle cure, but for the first time in my life, I had overcome rejection without pills and a spell in hospital. Several months passed and Janet came back into my life which was the worst thing that could've happened. I had moved to student accommodation on the Quayside in Newcastle by then to be closer to the university.

The same old things started to happen again with her not turning up or making excuses. Then one day after drinking myself into oblivion, I found my old bottle of tranquillizers and swallowed as many as possible until collapsing in a heap. I must have hit the floor with a loud bang because in the early hours of the morning, the police kicked my door in and had me taken to Newcastle's Freeman hospital. I had my stomach pumped and was observed for several days. However, Janet not being satisfied that I had gone as low as I could came to visit me just to finish me off. It was the last time I ever saw her as I walked her to the entrance. She had met someone else I later heard, but I hadn't lost a loving partner. I'd had a lucky escape and was much better off without her. I've no idea why she felt the need to come and see me in hospital. Perhaps it made her feel good about herself.

But I had been through the mill and it had taken its toll. With no energy left or fight inside of me, I did what I had done in prison when Tina had driven me to despair. I turned to my books and got back to my studies where I sailed through my second year and was now on my way to completing my degree. I still continued to go from one bad relationship to another but never getting as deeply involved as I had with Janet.

My behaviour never changed really and I continued to drink too much. I hit a bad patch again when I met another girl called Lisa who was twelve years younger than me. After my ordeal with Janet, I never went out with an older woman again. I wasn't going to pay the price for how badly other men had treated them anymore.

Lisa had a weird relationship with her father and sometimes when we went out for a drink - I had to spend the night in the pub with both of them. She was twenty-five-years-old, yet would go on the town with her father more than anyone else. They would sit there hardly saying a word to me. It was like pulling teeth. There was something very odd about the whole family. It could only end in disaster and after a massive fall out, I decided it was time to head back to Teesside. I transferred my degree course to Teesside University and for the first time since leaving prison two years earlier, I actually began to settle.

CHAPTER TWENTY THREE

THE PEN IS MIGHTIER THAN THE SWORD

In 2001, I graduated from Teesside University with a bachelor's degree in criminology. Graduation day was the proudest moment of my life and my mother was overjoyed. My mother and Donald both came to the ceremony. I felt the same buzz of excitement I had the day I was released from prison. Then the following year, I started my master's degree. Donald was always joining in at home advising me and giving me the benefit of his wealth of knowledge.

They were enjoyable times and Donald's passion for learning was infectious as it always had been when he first tried to help me study for a GCSE in law back in 1987. Indeed, other things have led me on to my path of learning. For example, there was the Durham prison officer, Mr Coates who had put me on education classes in 1984 which led to my first ever qualification. Then there was the inspiring autobiography of bank robber, turned journalist and postgraduate, John McVicar.

My mother who had attended college for years studying music, encouraged me to continue my studies I'd started in Durham prison, which made me take up a psychology 'O' level course at *Redcar College* in 1985. Then there were the lifers I had spent so much time with in prison who had a massive influence on me and my journey into prison education and writing. But once I had reached university, it was ultimately Donald's influence, passion for learning, his endless knowledge, support and encouragement that drove me on to complete my degrees. Then half way through my master's degree, Donald died aged eighty-one years old. It was the worst blow I had ever had and I was devastated at the loss of my soul mate. It was the first family bereavement of a close relative I had ever experienced. And ever since then, I have never been able to return to higher education since completing my master's degree in 2003, albeit there have been many attempts.

But though I grieved and felt depressed for a long time after Donald's death, I never turned to anti-depressants. He would never see me graduate the second time around, or ever know I had entered the world of journalism he'd been a great part of most of his life. But in his honour I continued to work on a book he wrote which to date is soon to be published. One of my lecturers used to tell me that education is a great leveller and for me, this is so true. However, for the first two years of being in Higher Education - as I have explained - I lead a life of self destruction and mayhem, as well as abusing all the faith people had put in me. For those first two years after being set free, I struggled to resettle back into society.

Trying to settle into university life during my resettlement period from prison put a huge strain on me. But eventually, it started to pay off. Most of society can accept the folly of youth as a reason for going off the rails - depending on the severity of the crimes of course. In most cases, a young person can still turn things around. But for me, this didn't happen until I was in my thirties leaving myself an almost impossible task to start afresh. I remember thinking, 'How can I ever justify my actions now?' After my first stint in prison when I was in my twenties maybe, but not in my thirties. Most will agree that we can all make mistakes when we are young and irresponsible and that people eventually mature - right? But surely after a certain age, aren't you just a lost cause? I mean how do you convince people you deserve a third, fourth, fifth, sixth or umpteenth chance? Can you ever change after a certain age? What is the age deadline where society will stop accepting your past actions as having been those of someone who was at the time, 'young and daft?', or, 'He just made a mistake?' Surely I'd blown any chance of being rehabilitated now?

Having a criminal record when I was younger was a burden when it came to employment, but in those days, unless you revealed your convictions to your interviewer - or someone informed on you, you could get into most jobs because in those days, there was no Criminal Records Bureau. Now with almost all employers requesting CRB checks, things have changed and made it more difficult for ex-offenders to play down their past. It's not that we should tell lies and deliberately hide our past, but those who committed relatively minor offences way back, should not be subjected to being judged based on the limited information a CRB reveals.

I gave up on the employment market many years ago and went along the self employed route instead which was in fact, one of the best decisions I'd ever made. My regrets are that I wasn't encouraged to work hard at education early in life. If I had been, I may have turned out a very different person.

After my degrees ended, I re-ignited my passion for writing from all those years ago when I used to type away in Acklington for hours a day in my cell - writing down my thoughts and feelings on paper. It's a good feeling that I've since been able to use these skills to help others by promoting their businesses, raising issues on people's behalves and running news writing workshops. I now work as a full time author, journalist and guest lecturer - enjoying every minute of it. So many things have come full circle for me. But nothing could have gone as full circle than when I was sat in a courtroom at York in 2007 reporting on a case for the York Press - the very courts I myself was a defendant in over twenty years before. And writing for the very newspaper that had once reported my first crime and myself as a wanted man.

The former Chief Inspector of prisons, Sir David Ramsbotham, once said that communication is the scourge of the twenty-first-century and that prisons are full of people who are not very good at communicating effectively or appropriately. Thankfully, I had not only learned to do this through writing which became a way of life and a necessity, but also by talking and not bottling things up inside.

I had massive social inhibitions during my life. I was incapable of communicating effectively with people properly from a very young age. So I was always acting, always trying to be somebody else. Being unable to communicate properly can cause frustration and anger, so at times lashing out seems the most appropriate solution. I learned that having the ability to communicate, meant I was able to get my message across in a civilised manner.

In prison, I would often get requests to write letters for inmates to their loved ones or solicitors, or help others with their Open University work. I became a useful person to know and it was nice to be able to help others who couldn't read or write very well. I helped in any way I could. I was even asked by the prisoner's forum to write the minutes for their meetings. It was all good practice and hopefully went some way to helping others. It also showed me that I had a skill that I could one day put to good use. For me, writing is what I do best. This is what helped me to initially self analyse my inner most feelings. During my tough times in prison with Tina, I would spend hours writing down my thoughts and emotions.

I believe it was my writing that helped me get parole despite several good reasons why I should not have got it. I did this by putting across a good argument what I intended to do to change things. It was my writing that landed me a place at university and it was my writing that has since earned me a living and enabled me to pen my life story to share to the world.

Such is the power of the written word I even used my writing skills to convince the judge to sentence me to a lesser prison term of five years from what he originally had planned for me. I know this because while in Wealstun, I decided to write a letter to him.

In my letter, I reminded him of the two sides of A4 paper I had written to the court expressing my deepest, darkest feelings and how I had allowed 'my emotions to get the better of me.' And how I had continued to do what I had said I would do and as a result been offered a place at university. I was stunned when I received a reply from him expressing his delight that I had kept to my word. I felt completely humbled that he had taken the time to respond with a handwritten letter that read,

Dear Mr Honeywell, Thank you for writing to me. After reading your letter I referred to my notebook for 15 December 1995 and was reminded of the circumstances in which I sentenced you to five years in prison. It was a serious case and you had a bad record. Your letter to the court which you now remind me I made reference to in passing sentence, permitted me to pass a shorter sentence than I had intended ...

If there ever was an example of how mighty the pen is - this was it. Donald tried many times to prove to me that the 'pen was mightier than the sword' - that words are a much more powerful tool than a fist or a knife.

When people believe in you, it makes the world of difference. But I really must emphasise that in my opinion, prison does not work. Only self change can turn things around. In 1993 - the home secretary at the time - Michael Howard famously announced that 'Prison works.'

Of course we have seen in many cases that nothing could be further from the truth. Prison can only work if a person can make it work for them by realising how much of a 'mugs game' it is - by using their time as constructively as possible. And by reflecting and planning their route to changing things.

The authorities naturally think that I'm an example of how prison works and that my success is attributed to being in prison. Granted, had I not been in prison, I doubt I would have passed my OU course. But ultimately, the decision to change came from inside my soul.

During the first two years after being released, it was obvious that having a place at university wasn't enough on its own to change me - and that I was in fact far from being rehabilitated. For I now realised that I had to look deep within myself if I was ever to stand any chance of changing. All I had done so far was create the tools which could open doors - the rest was up to me.

CHAPTER TWENTY FOUR

MY JOURNEY TO
SELF CHANGE

B eing able to prove to others that you have changed can be a frustrating and endless battle. Only those who have changed truly know if they have or not. I have many regrets and I as I said at the beginning, if I could change things I would. But what does it have to actually take before society - including the police and other organisations accept that one has changed?

I always knew I had issues with alcohol and had I dealt with this early in life, things would be very different now. Of course, there was always my underlying mental health problems, but I had always tried to get help for this. I was fully aware I needed help and always sought it out.

During my life, I have seen approximately ten different psychiatrists for depression, two of who were forensic psychiatrists who specialise in working with the criminal mind. I had also begged my GP doctor for counselling, but I tired of the lengthy waiting lists and eventually gave up. I would always ask for help when I was at my worst state of mind; otherwise, they felt there was no need for me to be referred to a counsellor.

Had it not been for Fred's persistence that night he took me to York's Bootham psychiatric hospital, I would not have been admitted. The ignorance surrounding depression is still rife. People still think that everyone gets depressed - that you should, 'snap out of it', or 'pull yourself together'. I wonder how many times this was said to someone just before they took their own life. Those who commit suicide are viewed as cowards by many. But I can say for sure, it takes a brave person to take their own life. I do agree that those who intend to do it don't usually announce it, they just do it. Those who announce it are usually crying out for help and if so, then why ridicule them? If people need help to the extent of self-harming, then they should be given support.

It has taken me years of self analysis in an attempt to change and I still have to work very hard at it. Many of my inner scars will be there forever. And sometimes when I'm emotional, my behaviour can seem a little odd. The difference now is that I'm fully aware of it and can always bring myself back down to earth. I can attribute this ability to a lifetime of introspection and aging.

It wasn't until I was able to accept guilt and learn remorse; I was able to start changing my behaviour. Deep down I wish my entire criminal background could be wiped clean so that I could now be allowed to live a normal life. I know deep down that I no longer have those criminal urges I used to have, nor do I live a dysfunctional life. I maintain that my criminality was born out of being emotionally and mentally disturbed. It's clear that I was never a career criminal, nor had the capacity to be one.

I believe I have a lot to offer and could give a lot of useful advice to younger people and criminal justice organisations. Rehabilitated criminals in my view should be given the opportunity to give something back; otherwise a lot of real experiences which could be put to good use are wasted. If one person can benefit from a reformed criminal's experiences which gives the youth of today an insight into what may lie ahead for them, then it's worth giving them the opportunity to offer this help.

Recently, I met my former probation officer, Russell Bruce, now Chief Executive Officer of Durham Tees Valley Probation Trust. It was twenty-eight-years since we first met and I had mixed emotions of both intrigue and yet sadness. Although I was looking forward to meeting him again, I was able to tell him that I eventually made good. But I was sad because it had taken me so many years to do so.

We have both come a long way since 1983 when I committed my first offence and Russell was new to his profession. But the thing I found most intriguing, was that although we both took very different paths, we both met up at the other end having succeeded in our chosen careers. Had I listened to Russell all those years ago, I may not have had to endure twenty years of misery and uphill struggle to reach my goals.

Probation back then was very much focused on rehabilitation which seems to be a dirty word to a lot of the public now. But it should never be forgotten that some offenders can change and will if the tools are made available to them. I had an inability to communicate when I was a youth, so I used to bottle things up. But after developing my communicating skills through writing and learning to talk, communicating would one day become my career.

Once I realised that the relationship between probation officer and offender wasn't an 'us and them' scenario after all, I started to trust them and then started to improve. And due to all my probation officers commitment to helping me and their unwavering empathy, I was able to work with them through all of my problems. The most powerful thing I found was that no matter what happened, they would always look at things optimistically.

When I was going through a particularly tough time with Janet and I'd had an altercation with the police, I turned up for my weekly appointment with my probation officer in North Shields - looking as though I'd been in a car crash. Expecting her to look horrified - instead, she just acted like it was just another glitch that could be ironed out. I even begged them to recall me back to prison; such was my state of mind at the time. But no matter how much I tried to demonstrate how much of a lost cause I was who just needed to be locked up, they would not have me recalled, or give up on me.

Battered and bruised, I tried to plead with her boss who I spotted leaning against the doorway having a cigarette one day. He just looked at me and said, 'You can still turn this around you know.' I couldn't see it and I was so frustrated that I wasn't getting through to them. But thanks to their unshakable faith in me and persistence in making me see that all I had to do to change was alter my behavioural pattern and to learn better communication skills, I eventually did. And the probation officer at North Shields, who told me things could be turned around, was right. I have lost count of the probation officers I have worked with over the years, but several stick in my mind who I worked with while in prison, during parole and on licence. And I can't fault any of them.

When my last probation order eventually came to an end and I broke all ties with them - I have to say - I did feel a sudden loss - as though something very special had ended. Perhaps it was the support network or just being able to pick up the phone anytime I wanted to speak to them. The meetings always involved lengthy discussions which was the best therapy of all. It was their counselling approach that really boosted me.

As I have said, rehabilitation must come from within, but a support network is vital. Most of all though, acceptance by society is essential. Fourteen years since leaving prison, I have come out of the cold to share my story in the hope that I can help others. The acceptance from my fellow academics as well as friends and family has made my journey so much easier. I should also mention that health and fitness has played a massive part in helping my mental health. I discovered many years ago the benefits exercise can have on the mind and body and how it alleviates many of the symptoms I used to get. I had learned about this when I was much younger but never appreciated it until I was older.

Even during my time in prison, the gym was an essential part of keeping myself emotionally stable. Even in an environment like that, you could get that 'feel good factor' after a session at the gym. It just helped the days go by a little easier. I had always used the gym from school age right through to today, but the demon drink had in the past always spoiled things for me. Physically, exercise gave me confidence while mentally it kept depression away - at least until I drank alcohol.

It was always a combination of things though that triggered my depression. Alcohol, although disastrous, was only part of a catalogue of problems. It would always start with a rejection of some kind, or a problem I felt unable to control, followed by binge drinking, followed by a criminal act. And it was this behavioural pattern I needed to break in order to self change.

Had it not been for my appetite for consuming large quantities of alcohol, I would have been more likely to maintain equilibrium of a healthy mind and healthy body, but once depression hits you, you can't think logically about things like exercise. Most days, you can't even bring yourself to get out of bed. Through the passage of time and with the inevitable transformation into maturity, I can now drink alcohol moderately. My life has been a journey of trying to correct things that I had blown in the past such as when I joined the territorial SAS in an attempt to rectify my failings in the 'regular army'.

I also regained credibility in education after leaving school with no qualifications. Then in 2007 I became a qualified fitness instructor and though my criminal past is a massive hindrance for me ever to work in the health and fitness industry, I give help wherever I can. I took the level two fitness instructor course at *Redcar College* which was where I had first attempted it back in 1984 but never completed.

My tutor Steve Brunskill was not only an inspirational teacher, but has continued to stay in touch and has become a good friend too. It hasn't just been about gaining degrees and university status, but also gaining other qualifications and learning new skills along the way.

Career-wise, my degrees have done little to help me, but psychologically, they have helped me beyond belief. Education as a whole has given me a new confidence I never had. It has focused my mind and taught me to think laterally and to question. However, most of all, education has taught me that no matter how difficult life becomes; you can find a way out through sheer determination. I don't believe any one thing can be attributed to desistance from crime. It has to be an accumulation of things, education being only one of them. Achieving my fitness qualification not only continued my journey of learning which has now become a necessity in my life, but I also gained a good, professional knowledge on how to maintain a healthy lifestyle.

This qualification alongside my own experiences has helped me enormously and I am even able to put my cooking skills to good use through my knowledge of healthy eating. Not all offenders want to go to university and not all have the basis to get into university. But there are other educational pathways to one's own rehabilitation. For some, it may be higher education, but for others it can be just learning how to lead a healthier and more constructive life away from drugs and alcohol. Not all education is about gaining qualifications.

My fitness training started at fifteen with regular running and weight training which all centred around masculinity. I started weight training because I was bullied at school and wanted to increase in size. As I have matured, it has become more of a necessity both mentally and physically. Mentally it releases endorphins that give me that 'feel good factor' and physically, I feel proud to be in good shape as I approach my fifties.

For years, I had depended on anti-depressants, but the best therapy of all was an accumulation of regular exercise, hobbies and interests and setting myself long-term goals.

Martial arts played an important role later in life too. I find it strange that some parents won't send their children to martial arts classes because they believe it teaches them violence. On the contrary, learning violence is the last thing martial arts teach a person. A person learns martial arts because they don't want to fight, not because they want do. And the big egos are soon shown the door by any good sensei (instructor).

Martial arts for me, was a way to learn how to deal with violence in a diplomatic way. My use of knives was because I was never adept at using my fists. Martial arts teach you to do this as a last resort. But ultimately, it teaches you how to avoid violence and develop an awareness of danger. And most importantly not to feel inadequate walking away from a fight.

In 2008, I gained a black belt 'first dan' in aikido. Aikido is purely self defence and I found that it made my confidence grow even more. I believe that if I had learned martial arts to this level when I was younger, I would not have carried knives, or felt the need to use them. Aikido also has a spiritual side to it which I found very beneficial.

I still have my dark moments as everyone does. I go through phases where I get desperately upset about what I have done to others and myself in the past and how I wish I could turn the clock back. Don't we all? Whenever I see myself exceeding what I feel is sensible drinking, I pull back and get myself back on track. Alcohol is the one thing that can bring my personality disorder to the surface and make me behave oddly.

As I have grown older, in one way, I have become less tolerant of society and in another way, more tolerant. I think I have just learned to give my time and energy to what's most important and discard what isn't. I can socialise easily now and appreciate the simpler things in life. However, I have no patience with mindless 'thugishness', nor do I suffer fools. I sometimes wonder if I have any right to take this stance having been a 'thug' myself at times. Perhaps I see myself in 'thugs' and despise myself even more than I do them.

I continue to self-analyse and self-change as it isn't something that just ends - it's a continual life journey. And along the way you learn more about yourself and others. The underlying problems that caused my personality disorder remain. I have merely learned to manage them. But then I have the continual support of others who continue to tell me that I must forgive myself. This is one thing I can't achieve fully. But I will continue to pass my knowledge on to young people and show them what may await them if they choose to go along the wrong path. And how you end up when you have nothing left. Perhaps I can't achieve everything I want to, but I know I can and still have much work to do for myself and for others.

PRISON GLOSSARY

Inmate/Con/Lag .... Prisoner.
Screw .... Prison officer.
Block .... Solitary.
Slop out .... Disposing of human waste.
Bird/Porridge/Stretch/Doing Time .... Sentence.
R.O.Ps .... Restriction of privileges.
Lifer .... Life sentence prisoner.
Nonce/beast .... Sex offender.
Baccy/Burn/Snout .... Tobacco.
Scran .... Food.
Duff .... Pudding.
Pad .... A cell.
Spin .... A search (as in 'pad-spin').
Burglars .... Security or 'DST'
('Dedicated Search Team').
Bang up .... Time locked in cell.
Midnight .... Midnight mass - grass.
Ghosting ....Transferred   to another
prison, suddenly and without notice.
L-Plates .... A life sentence.
Cucumbers/Numbers/Protection ....'Nonces'
or 'Bacons' (sex offenders) and other 'Protection heads'
(debtors, grasses, cell thieves etc.) are usually segregated
for their own safety under Prison Rule 45 (formerly 43).
They should not be confused with prisoners held in the
block (the segregation unit) under Prison Rule 45 GOAD
(Good Order and Discipline).
Patches .... A prison uniform
with prominent yellow panels worn by prisoners captured
after an escape or following an attempted escape.
Pie and liquor ....The vicar